THE RIGHT TO WORK

Everyone has the right to work, to free choice of employment, to just and favourable conditions of work and to protection against unemployment.

Everyone, without any discrimination, has the right to equal pay for equal work.

Everyone who works has the right to just and favourable remuneration ensuring for himself and his family an existence worthy of human dignity, and supplemented if necessary, by other means of social protection.

Everyone has the right to form and to join trade unions for the protection of his interests.

Everyone has the right to rest and leisure, including reasonable limitation of working hours and periodic holidays with pay.

Universal Declaration of Human Rights, Articles 23 and 24

THE RIGHT TO WORK

The Loss of our First Freedom

edited by
Ken Coates MEP
with chapters by
Michael Barratt Brown
John Hughes
John Wells

SPOKESMAN
for
EUROPEAN LABOUR FORUM

First published in Great Britain in 1995 by
Spokesman
Bertrand Russell House
Gamble Street
Nottingham, England
Tel. 0115 9708318
Fax. 0115 9420433

British Library Cataloguing in Publication Data available on request from
the British Library.

ISBN 0-85124-577-3
ISBN 0-85124-578-1 pbk

Printed by the Russell Press Ltd, Nottingham
(Tel. 0115 9784505)

CONTENTS

CHAPTER ONE

The Loss of our First Freedom

Ken Coates MEP

All over Europe unemployment still rages at crisis levels. It becomes difficult to recall that, following the turmoil of the Second World War, once the European economies re-established themselves, there began an age of almost full employment, which endured for nearly three decades. By the 1970s, the unemployment statistics averaged between two and three per cent in all the countries of the European Community. But this figure had doubled by the beginning of the 1980s, and it almost doubled again by 1985. At that time it stood at eleven per cent of the employed workforce.

Nine million new jobs were engendered in the second half of the '80s, with the economic recovery which followed 1985. But the unemployment rate had only fallen to eight per cent by 1990, and it then rose steadily. By September 1994 it again reached 10.8 per cent, a total of more than eighteen million people out of work.

In 1993 employment overall had gone down by 1.8 per cent: the worst fall in the history of the European Community. 1994 maintained this trend, at a more relaxed pace. Preliminary estimates put the fall in that year at 0.6 per cent.

All these trends are very clear, even if the statistical evidence which is used to establish them is sometimes inadequate, even corrupt. John Wells has shown how far the British statistics are polluted, and his testimony has not been effectively challenged by any of the army of apologists who seek to minimise the scope of the problem in the United Kingdom. His evidence is reinforced by that of John Hughes, who has shown a similar level of pollution in the *em*ployment statistics.

For Britain, unemployment has become a veritable crucifixion of millions of people, who are excluded from every aspect of normal living. The incidence of long-term unemployment gives us new indices of misery: deprivation, poverty, family breakdown, loss of hope and self-esteem. Large tracts of Britain become dependent, hanging by their fingernails on the edge of a society which organises itself in carboot sales, those triumphs of the free market.

There arises a culture of extreme alienation. This borders on crime, and sometimes overlaps with it. The statistical evidence about this vital area of social pathology has once again been assembled and analysed by Dr Wells, in a truly forensic paper. It has become fashionable to threaten 'to be tough on crime, tough on the causes of crime'. But it is much easier to seek vengeance on those who are subject to poverty and rejection, whether they commit crimes or suffer from their commission, than it is to remove the roots of their distress. Without full employment, Dr Wells will persuade us, there will be a continuous supply of young criminals, with the continuous multiplication of victims and disruption of social standards.

John Hughes' examination of the collapse of full-time employment for the younger generation shows how bad this situation already is. There were fewer than 600,000 young workers aged under twenty-one in full-time employment, in April 1994. This represents a dreadful shrinkage, even within the present half decade. In April 1990 there had been almost one and a third million such young people with full-time jobs. Three quarters of a million jobs for youngsters have thus disappeared in a four year period: a loss of fifty-six per cent. It is impossible for society to survive the wholesale exclusion of its own young people from the normal processes of its life, just as it is impossible that mass unemployment can cohabit with social justice. The only justice which is admitted in this cruel universe is very primitive: raw, red in tooth and claw.

What justice can there be for the excluded? What are the claims of those who are not wanted in the labour market, not solvent in their own right, excluded from the active economy, and from ever widening areas of social life? Where is 'opportunity' on the dole? And 'equality', in a society which is polarised to a degree which none living can remember in their past?

Mass unemployment is the grave digger of democracy. Among youth, unemployment normally runs at double the proportion afflicting the workforce at large. Who can be surprised at the growth of xenophobia, random violence, petty and not so petty crime? The extreme right flourishes in this poisonous soil. Even more widely, cynicism grows. And solidarity? This is a good word, but where is it in the official political space of states which have come to live with the 'inevitable' fact that millions of their citizens must be excluded, either in perpetuity, or at least for many years? Let us not forget that today we are three times richer, on average, than we were when all of Europe enjoyed full employment. There is no excuse for locking one single human soul outside the gates.

Unemployment does not only hit those who have no jobs.

True: the unemployment regime drives millions into direct poverty, and excludes them from access to many basic amenities. But it also impacts with full force on those who retain their jobs: unless they possess especial skills, they find their own position undermined, and with this weakening goes loss of self-esteem. It becomes greatly more difficult for people to defend their rights. In that context, the rights themselves die back, and we reach a regressive state, in which things which yesterday were assumed must now be proved, and in which the weakest go to the wall.

Full employment, by contrast, changes the balance of power between employers and their workpeople. Even before an employee decides to join a trade union, he gains an advantage from the establishment of a sellers' market for labour. The security which this brings gives the employee the right to say 'no'. If an employer makes unreasonable demands, or offers unacceptably low rewards, or is too arbitrary and inconsiderate, then there is another job down the road, round the corner. It is no longer necessary to bite one's tongue.

In such circumstances, trade unions may flourish. A wide range of issues become 'management prerogatives' in times of high unemployment. The boss can call the shots, not only on levels of wages, but also on working time, the pattern and rhythm of work and the security of employment itself. High unemployment figures make dismissal a much feared penalty. Those who fear the sack, lose the ability to answer back. Fear imposes docility, which is often misinterpreted as contentment. Full employment dissolves this threat, and brings a situation in which workers enjoy something closer to freedom than is ever available to them in times of mass unemployment.

That is why, after the Second World War, full employment was recognised as the corner-stone of domestic economic policy in Britain, and as a founding principle of the Universal Declaration of Human Rights adopted by the United Nations in 1948. This read:

Art. 23:
(i) Everyone has the right to work, to free choice of employment, to just and favourable conditions of work and to protection against unemployment.
(ii) Everyone, without any discrimination, has the right to equal pay for equal work.
(iii) Everyone who works has the right to just and favourable remuneration ensuring for himself and his family an existence worthy of human dignity, and supplemented if necessary, by other means of social protection.
(iv) Everyone has the right to form and to join trade unions for the

protection of his interests.
Art. 24
Everyone has the right to rest and leisure, including reasonable limitation
of working hours and periodic holidays with pay.

Back in the age of full employment, all this was taken for granted.
The same commitment was endorsed by the signatories of the
Treaty of Rome. The Keynesian methods of demand management
made possible a redistributive regime, which by a combination of
taxation and borrowing, could quite effectively manage demand.
Within this stable environment, multinational companies put down
healthy roots, and grew and grew. Soon they could avoid many
liabilities to corporation tax, by the device of transfer pricing, which
enabled them to accumulate their profits in friendly areas, and
minimise them where they would attract high levels of tax. More
multinational power was accompanied by faster deregulation, and
the loss of national leverage over macro-economic policy.

But a modified Keynesian regime could be restored at the
European level. It would entail a commitment to redistribute
resources from the richer to the poorer half of society. Of course,
the great increase in wealth which has accompanied the growth of
unemployment, has itself been very unequally distributed. To the
rich have gone the fruits: to the poor, the rinds.

'Unto everyone that hath shall be given, and he shall have abundance;
but from him that hath not shall be taken away even that which he hath.'

The regeneration of employment in Britain would be much easier
if it were done as part of a Europe-wide project. This was the
promise of the Delors White Paper on *Growth, Competitiveness and
Employment.* This turned on the need to create fifteen million new
jobs by the end of the twentieth century, in order to halve the level
of unemployment in Europe.

The effort to implement the Delors proposals is the subject of
another little book which will appear at the same time as this one:
Putting Europe Back to Work.

The Delors White Paper did not make simplistic assumptions.
The researchers who had underpinned it were perfectly aware that
there were very great differences in the circumstances which
applied in different Member States. Not only did individual
unemployment rates diverge between 22 per cent in Spain and 6
per cent in Portugal or the Western Laender of Germany, but the
underlying *em*ployment statistics diverged considerably as well.
Under-employment in rural areas varied from one state to the next,
even from one region to the next. Youth unemployment ran at a

Community average of 13.2 per cent, varying between 36.4 per cent in Spain and 4.7 per cent in Germany. Long-term unemployment has been falling in Spain and Portugal, but rising in Greece. The employment rate, the ratio of the number of people employed to the population of working age, ran at 58 per cent across Europe in 1993, compared with 70 or more per cent in the United States and Japan.

There were already many Community initiatives concerned with the need to minimise unemployment. During the Edinburgh summit which took place in December 1992, it was agreed to create new medium-term loan facilities, which would include the establishment of a European Investment Fund to guarantee and finance new projects. All twelve Member States subsequently ratified the necessary changes in the Treaty of Rome, to enable the European Community to borrow in its own right.

Following the Edinburgh Conference, the Commission presented its White Paper on *Growth, Competitiveness and Employment* to the European Council in December 1993. It recognised that present day unemployment included significant structural and technological components, and no longer simply reflected the movements of the trade cycle. To this extent, it would not yield to the normal processes of recovery from recession.

For this reason it would be necessary to initiate joint and combined action on major infrastructural works such as the Trans-European Networks in transport, communications, and energy. It would also be necessary to accelerate action to advance lifelong education and training, to assist small and medium enterprises, and to foster local employment creation.

The expenditures envisaged in the White Paper were considerable. It was suggested that the Trans-European Networks and kindred measures would involve investments rising from 150 billion ecus, over time, up to 550 billion ecus. The idea of the European Investment Fund was that it would enable active works on a large scale to be funded in what would effectively constitute a European Public Sector Borrowing Requirement. This would simultaneously generate new employment, and avoid the restraints on individual state budgets that had been agreed in the Maastricht Treaty, which were aimed at bringing the Member States into convergence, to assist the processes entailed in monetary union.

But the Essen summit in December 1994 did not agree to enlarge this European borrowing facility. In the awful jargon of Euro-speak, the expenditure on the Trans-European Networks was to be 'subsidiarised'. This means that it would be funded by national borrowing which would fall within the Maastricht convergence criteria, and thus displace other national infrastructural investments, rather than ride alongside them in an additional process.

Perhaps it is not surprising that 'Euro-Keynesianism' policies should be difficult to apply when the culture in all the European Member States is becoming more restrictive, conservative, and socially divisive. If even the left is parroting the language of dynamic market priorities, then, it may be thought there is no chance for the poor, or for the unemployed.

Can this be true? I think not. To continue to live with wholesale social exclusion, is to live with decline and disintegration. No-one can argue that such conditions are 'necessary'. A society which accepts them is sick, and the sickness cannot be defined by its symptom, which is unemployment. The sickness is in the heart of things, which must be changed.

CHAPTER TWO

The Missing Million

John Wells

The 602,000 fall in the UK's official unemployment measure — the claimant count of those unemployed and 'signing-on' for unemployment-related benefits — from its recent (January 1993) peak of 2.992 million came as a complete surprise to virtually everyone, including the entire economics profession — not a single member of which predicted it.

However, certain features of this fall in claimant unemployment raise doubts as to whether it really is indicating an improvement in labour market conditions. For example, the time-lag between output recovery in the non-oil economy (3Q 1992) and the February 1993 fall in claimant unemployment — just 6 months — is unusually short; during the previous 1980s cycle, claimant unemployment turned down in 1986, lagging by five years the output recovery (in 1981) and by three years the employment recovery (in 1983). Furthermore, the 602,000 fall in claimant unemployment is exceptionally large in relation to the maximum possible rise in employment that may have occurred: 408,000, according to the Labour Force Survey, largely self-employed and part-time employees, or 80,000 according to the Department of Employment's *Survey*; and reverses the past relationship in which reductions in unemployment are only a fraction of increases in employment as newly-employed workers are partly drawn from the 'inactive' reserve.

Such questions have re-opened long-standing doubts about the value of claimant unemployment, both as a measure of the level of unemployment and as an indicator of changes in labour market conditions. These stem partly from the 29 changes introduced into the UK's unemployment measure since 1979 — all of which have served either to depress the total or leave it unchanged; and partly from the performance targets set the Employment Service in respect of inflows onto and outflows from the count which, together with the 29 changes, raise the spectre of possible systemic administrative bias or 'fiddle' affecting the figures. An additional source of concern is the large mis-match during the early 1990s recession between reductions in employment (2 million) and increased claimant unemployment (just 1.4 million) — which, taking into account moderately expansionary demographic factors, meant that 826,600 people (632,400 men and 194,200 women) disappeared from the statisticians' gaze into 'inactivity'.

This article contends that the claimant count understates UK involuntary unemployment by at least one million. And, for this reason as well as others, it is unsatisfactory as an indicator of changes in labour market conditions.

Post-war unemployment in the UK: three official measures

Figure 1 plots post-war unemployment in the UK using three measures. Prior to 1982, unemployment was measured as a clerical record of those 'registered' as unemployed with the government's employment service (job centres and careers offices). Registrants were those accepted by employment services staff as being 'capable and available for work', whether they were entitled to unemployment benefit or not. Many factors affected the propensity of unemployed men and women to register, including their eligibility for benefit, whether they thought being on the register

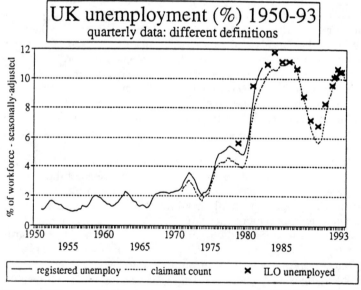

Figure 1: UK unemployment: percentage of workforce, 1950-93 — different definitions

would help them get a job, and so on. Thus, 'registered unemployed' was not intrinsically superior as a measure of unemployment to the clamaint count.

Introduced on November 11 1982, the 'clamaint' count of those unemployed and signing on for unemployment-related benefits at UBOs (Unemployment Benefit Offices) was a consequence of the Thatcher Government's Rayner administrative economy measures, which made registration/attendance at job-centres voluntary. Unemployment-related benefits are three in number; Unemployment Benefit (UB): a non-means-tested benefit, available to those meeting certain national insurance contributory conditions and presently available for 12 months, to be cut to six months from April 1996, when it is replaced by the Jobseekers' Allowance; Income Support (IS): a means-tested benefit available after UB has been exhausted due to long-duration unemployment or where a person is judged to have made him/herself voluntarily unemployed; and National Insurance credits (which those ineligible for UB or IS can 'sign on' for in order to satisfy contribution conditions, for example, for the state retirement pension). The claimant count resulted in an improvement in accuracy in certain respects — since it is mainly based on computerised records and has more up-to-date information on outflows from unemployment.

The third measure — ILO unemployment — is based on internationally-agreed guidelines and is derived from the results of the household *Labour Force Survey*. It is defined as 'those without a job (i.e. did not undertake more than one hour's work for pay or profit during the week prior to the interview), who were available to start work in the following two weeks and had either looked for work during the previous four weeks or were waiting to start a job already obtained'. ILO unemployment, which replaced so-called LF unemployment (more restrictive on the job search side [1 week as against 4] but lacking an availability condition and measured biannually 1979-83) has been estimated each Spring annually since 1984 and each quarter since 1992.

Claimant unemployment: its main shortcomings

'The count inevitably reflects the administrative system on which it is based and cannot be ideal for every purpose, for example, for measuring labour slack or social hardship'. *Employment Gazette*, October 1986, p.418

The main disadvantage of the claimant count as a measure of unemployment is that 'it is a by-product of an administrative system for paying benefits' (*Employment Gazette*, October 1992, p.456). It is a reflection, therefore, of that benefit system and, in particular, the rules governing unemployed peoples' eligibility for benefit. It is sensitive to changes affecting the administration or coverage of the benefit system as well as those of a purely statistical kind. Since 1979, UK unemployment has been subject to 29 changes — 24 counting from the switch to the claimant measure — all of which resulted in either a reduction or no change; although the Department of Employment (ED) only recognise eight of these changes as having had a significant effect on the count.

Two of the principal changes affected the old and the young unemployed, and discussing them in some detail illustrates how claimant unemployment understates the true unemployment total.

Changes introduced in 1981 and 1983 meant that unemployed people aged 60 and over (principally men), who were in receipt of Income Support or obtaining National Insurance credits, were no longer required to sign on; as a result, unemployed men aged 60 and over are only included on the claimant count if in receipt of UB. The official explanation for this change was that such men 'mostly considered themselves to be retired and were no longer required to sign on as available for work in order to receive benefit.' This purely administrative change resulted in a substantial reduction in the number of unemployed men aged 60 and over included in the claimant count: from 250,000 in 1983 to just 50,000 by mid-1993

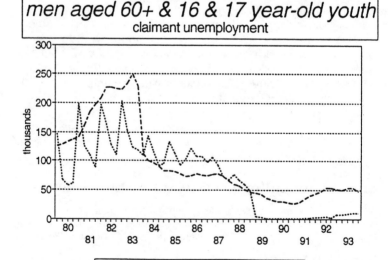

men aged 60+ & 16 & 17 year-old youth
claimant unemployment

Figure 2: Claimant unemployment amongst men aged 60+ and 16 & 17 year-old youths, 1979-93

Table 1
Men aged 60 and over, GB: employment and non-employment
(unemployment and inactivity rates), 1977-91

Year	ILO un-employed aged 60+	Registered/ claimant un-employed[1] aged 60+	Employ-ment rate 60-64 years	Non-employment rate 60-64 years	Of which ILO un-employed 60-64 years	Inactivity rate 60-64 years
	As % employed plus unemployed			as % population in age group		
1977	5.9	n.a.	73.7	26.3	5.3	21.0
1979	5.3	11.7	69.2	30.8	4.2	26.7
1981	9.0	16.8	61.9	38.1	7.7	30.4
1983	9.5	20.3	52.3	47.7	6.7	41.0
1984	8.6	8.1	51.2	48.8	5.4	43.4
1985	8.4	7.4	49.6	50.4	4.7	45.7
1986	8.5	7.6	48.1	51.9	4.8	47.1
1987	10.5	7.5	48.7	51.3	6.2	45.1
1988	9.1	5.3	48.9	51.1	5.7	45.4
1989	8.7	3.7	49.8	50.2	4.8	45.4
1990	8.1	2.9	49.3	50.7	5.0	45.7
1991	8.6	4.2	48.8	51.2	5.2	46.0

Source: *Employment Gazette* and *Labour Force Survey* (various).
Notes:
1. data for UK from 1981 onwards and for April (for comparability with Spring *LFS*).

(male unemployment overall standing at similar levels at these two dates): an effect which can be readily appreciated from Figure 2. By contrast, ILO unemployment amongst this group has remained roughly constant since 1983 (see Table 1).

However, both measures understate considerably the true degree of non-employment amongst older men: the employment rate amongst men aged 60-64 years has fallen sharply from 73.7% in 1977 to a point where less than half of the men in this age group (48.8% in 1991) now work. Increased non-employment is partly reflected in increased unemployment but, mainly, in increased inactivity. This, in turn, no doubt partly reflects a rise in voluntary early retirement. But, it mainly results from involuntary withdrawal from the labour market: in the wake of the massive destruction of male industrial jobs during the 1980s, men in this age group have given up all hope of finding work. They disappear statistically, being counted neither amongst claimant nor ILO unemployed.

Unemployed young workers have also virtually disappeared from the claimant count following the 1988 Social Security Act, which withdrew eligibility for Income Support (IS) from 16 and 17 year-old young people in most circumstances consequent upon the government's 'guarantee' to any young person not in full-time

Table 2
ILO and claimant unemployment and schooling rates amongst 16 & 17 year-olds, 1984-93

Year	ILO un-employment[1] (%) not s.a.	Claimant un-employment (%)	Population 000s	In full-time education 000s	Schooling rates (%)
Spring 1984	21.5	18.9	1814	689	38.0
Spring 1985	20.3	16.0	1769	671	37.9
Spring 1986	20.8	21.5	1730	663	38.3
Spring 1987	19.4	13.8	1700	655	38.5
Spring 1988	14.1	11.5	1688	668	40.0
Spring 1989	10.8	0.2	1641	680	41.4
Spring 1990	11.5	0.2	1537	689	44.8
Spring 1991	15.2	0.4	1491	706*	47.4*
Spring 1992	16.1	2.4	1426*	760*	53.3*
Summer 1992	23.3	2.0			
Autumn 1992	18.4	4.1	1307	866	66.3
Winter 1992/3	17.6	3.3	1300*	913*	70.2*

Source: calculated from *Employment Gazette, Labour Force Survey* and Department for Education, *Statistical Bulletin*.
Note:
1. ILO unemployment includes those in full-time education seeking part-time employment.
*ILO unemployment amongst those not in full-time education is slightly higher: 23.2% as against 18.4% in autumn 1992.

education or work to provide a place on the Youth Training Scheme. Figure 2 illustrates how this administrative change brought about the virtual disappearance of 16 and 17 year-old youths from the claimant count. However, the government's guarantee notwithstanding, ILO unemployment amongst this group has remained high — albeit cyclical (see Table 2). Thus, in Winter 1992/3, whilst only 15,800 16 & 17 year-olds were included on the claimant count (mainly those in receipt of Special Hardship Payments), the *Labour Force Survey* indicated that, of those 16 & 17 year-olds not in full-time education, 75,000 were ILO unemployed and a further 28,000 economically inactive; 50,000 in full-time education were also considered ILO unemployed — typically seeking part-time jobs. The official justification for excluding 16 & 17 year-olds from the claimant count is that their failure to take up a place on a Training Scheme renders them involuntarily unemployed. However, most 16 & 17 year-old young people must be assumed to start out on their working-lives wanting to work; the failure of Training and Enterprise Councils (TECs) to meet the training guarantee either quantitatively or qualitatively (meeting the aspirations of young people for good quality training)

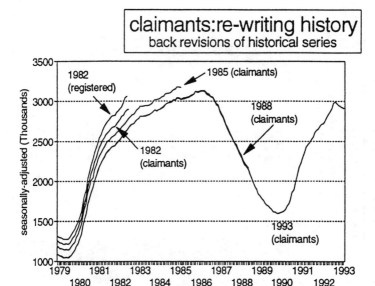

claimants:re-writing history
back revisions of historical series

Figure 3: UK claimant unemployment (men & women): back revisions to historical series

does not thereby render roughly 20 per cent of 16 & 17 year-olds voluntarily unemployed.

Claimant count and re-writing history

The 29 changes made to headline unemployment since 1979 raise the issue of how to generate an unemployment series on a consistent basis over time. The Employment Department (ED) attempts to solve this problem by computing and publishing periodically back revisions to the historical 'claimant' series on a basis consistent with the changing (reduced) coverage of the benefit regime. What this means in the case of a group whose eligibility to benefit has been withdrawn, or which is no longer required to sign on, is that the past numbers in that group are estimated and then subtracted from the historic totals. However, the ED does not take all 29 changes into account in its revisions — only those which it judges to have changed conditions of benefit eligibility, leaving aside changes thought irrelevant or insignificant: just eight altogether (see Figure 3).

Such changes now produce a very different version of unemployment history compared with contemporaneous perceptions of reality. Thus, for Spring 1981, registered

Table 3
Claimant and LFS/ILO unemployment compared: GB, seasonally-adjusted

Year	LF/ILO unemployed s.a. (millions)	% economically active (%)	Claimant unemployed (revised i.e. consistent with current coverage) (millions)	% workforce (%)	Announced unemployed (registered & claimants: changing coverage) (millions)	% workforce (%)
Spring 1979	1.44	5.6	1.046	4.0	1.26	5.3
Spring 1981	2.494	9.5	1.983	7.6	2.326	10.0
Spring 1983	2.865	11.0	2.663	10.3	2.894	12.4
Spring 1984	2.928	11.1	2.777	10.5	2.899	12.3
Spring 1984	3.105	11.7	2.777	10.5	2.899	12.3
Spring 1985	2.98	11.1	2.885	10.8	3.047	12.9
Spring 1986	2.981	11.1	3.000	11.0	3.077	11.4
Spring 1987	2.89	10.6	2.799	10.3	2.878	10.6
Spring 1988	2.385	8.6	2.269	8.2	2.341	8.5
Spring 1989	1.983	7.1	1.741	6.4	1.765	6.3
Spring 1990	1.871	6.6	1.5	5.4	1.51	5.4
Spring 1991	2.30	8.2	2.064	7.5	2.07	7.5
Spring 1992	2.649	9.5	2.578	9.4	2.578	9.4
Summer 1992	2.758	9.9	2.658	9.7	2.658	9.7
Autumn 1992	2.837	10.3	2.767	10.1	2.767	10.1
Winter 1992/3	2.931	10.6	2.87	10.5	2.87	10.5
Spring 1993	2.839	10.3	2.827	10.4	2.827	10.4
Summer 1993	2.854	10.3	2.814	10.3	2.814	10.3
Autumn 1993	2.809	10.1	2.753	10.0	2.753	10.0
Winter 1993/4	2.729	9.9	2.672	9.8	2.672	9.8
Spring 1994	2.650	9.6	2.589	9.5	2.589	9.5
Summer 1994	2.637	9.5	2.525	9.4	2.525	9.4
Autumn 1994	2.492	9.0	2.421	9.0	2.421	9.0

Source: *Labour Force Survey* (various) and *Employment Gazette* (various).

unemployment announced at the time was 2.328 million, and from the *Labour Force Survey* 2.494 million; but the revised claimant count now yields 1.984 million (see Table 3) — a difference of 510,000 compared with the 1981 *Labour Force Survey*!

The ED defends its procedure mainly by criticising the alternative approach, namely attempting to assess what unemployment would be on a previous basis of measurement — for example, prior to the 29 changes (the approach adopted by the Unemployment Unit — see below). 'Any attempt to assess what unemployment would now be on an old definition involves speculation about the effect of demographic and economic change and other factors. For instance . . . the introduction of voluntary registration and the changes since then, including changes in the labour market and the role played by jobcentres, make *meaningless* any attempt to estimate the number who would now be registered as unemployed on the old definition. Similarly, not least given the sharp fall in the number of young people into the early 1990s, it would be unrealistic to continue estimating unemployment on the coverage of the count prior to September 1988.' (*Gazette*, December 1988, p.661)

These arguments are far from persuasive. For example, whilst there is considerable difference in practice between obtaining past data on 16 and 17 year-old claimants and deleting them from previous totals, and trying to unearth (from, for example, the *Labour Force Survey*) data on 16 & 17 year-old unemployed non-claimants, they are completely symmetrical activities. However, the former (ED) approach eliminates information and re-writes a group out of the historical record simply because of an administrative change, whilst the latter highlights new information.

Moreover, regardless of any shortcomings of an alternative approach, the case *against* the ED's procedure could be overwhelming. Namely, that this exercise in re-writing history — even if not on quite the scale of Orwell's *1984* — compounds existing doubts regarding the legitimacy of the claimant count.

The Unemployment Unit index

The Unemployment Unit (UU), a registered charity campaigning for full employment policies, in their attempt to compute a consistent unemployment series over time, asks what unemployment would be prior to the 29 changes.

When the UU index is plotted against the claimant count, the UU index is higher everywhere — with the gap growing absolutely and relatively over time. According to the UU index, unemployment

in October 1993 stood at 4m against the official count of 2.86m —
more than 1m or nearly 40% higher: a significant difference.

In coming to a judgement concerning the merits of the UU index,
it is not possible to defend every aspect of its methodology in detail.
It obviously involves some rather rough-and-ready procedures.
Moreover, there is no reason to treat the pre-claimant 'registered'
basis for measuring unemployment as an absolute 'gold standard'
— given the existence of large numbers of non-registered
unemployed.

However, the fact that the UU Index is running at a far higher
level than the official claimant count does raise an obvious question:
is unemployment under three million, as measured by the claimant
count, or is it closer to four million, as estimated by the UU index?

Comparing claimant and ILO unemployment

The claimant count appears able to summon in its support the ILO
measure of unemployment. Claimant unemployment and ILO
unemployment coincide quite closely (see Table 3 and Figure 1)
— at least in total and from 1986 onwards.

Such agreement may be a source of re-assurance for some — or,
alternatively, a surprise for others, given the quite distinct
approaches to measuring unemployment which each embodies.
The agreement between the two is even more surprising, given that
they comprise such different populations.

Common to both ILO and claimant unemployment, there exists
a core of people unemployed on both definitions: ILO unemployed
claimants (see Table 4) — a group which is cyclically-sensitive. ILO
unemployed claimants would be included in any generally-agreed
measure of unemployment. However, ILO unemployed claimants
account for only about two-thirds of total unemployment measured
under either approach — 1.82 million out of a total of 2.8 million
(summer 1993).

In addition to this common core, ILO unemployment comprises
ILO unemployed non-claimants, i.e. those who are unemployed
according to the ILO criteria but are not eligible to sign on for
unemployment-related benefits and do not, therefore, appear on
the claimant count. In summer 1993, there were 1.08 million ILO
unemployed non-claimants (see Table 5).

Claimant unemployment, on the other hand, comprises, in
addition to ILO unemployed claimants, a group of claimants not
considered ILO unemployed, because either in employment or
economically inactive according to ILO criteria. In summer 1993,
one million claimants were considered not ILO unemployed.

Table 4
ILO and claimant unemployment: composition compared: men & women, GB, not seasonally-adjusted (millions)

| Year | ILO unemployed total | ILO unemployed non-claimants | ILO unemployed claimants | Claimant unemployed not-ILO unemployed | | | Total claimant |
				Econ-inactive	In employment	Total	
Spring 1983	2.91	0.76	2.15	0.67	0.17	0.84	2.98
Spring 1984	2.90	0.87	2.04	0.74	0.20	0.94	2.99
Spring 1984	3.09	0.87	2.22	0.58	0.18	0.76	2.98
Spring 1985	2.97	0.84	2.13	0.81	0.19	1.00	3.13
Spring 1986	2.97	0.81	2.16	0.82	0.19	1.01	3.17
Spring 1987	2.88	0.84	2.04	0.73	0.18	0.91	2.95
Spring 1988	2.38	0.77	1.60	0.62	0.19	0.81	2.41
Spring 1989	1.98	0.85	1.13	0.44	0.21	0.65	1.78
Spring 1990	1.87	0.86	1.01	0.32	0.19	0.51	1.52
Spring 1991	2.30	0.89	1.42	0.40	0.26	0.66	2.08
Spring 1992	2.65	0.89	1.76	0.53	0.32	0.85	2.61
Summer 1992	2.80	1.01	1.79	0.59	0.28	0.88	2.67
Autumn 1992	2.80	0.98	1.82	0.56	0.35	0.91	2.74
Winter 92/3	2.92	0.99	1.93	0.63	0.36	0.99	2.92
Spring 93	2.80	0.95	1.86	0.62	0.38	1.00	2.86
Summer 93	2.89	1.08	1.82	0.67	0.33	1.00	2.81
Autumn 93	2.79	1.04	1.76	0.61	0.36	1.00	2.72
Winter 93/4	2.74	0.99	1.75	0.63	0.36	0.99	2.74
Spring 94	2.62	0.96	1.65	0.61	0.37	0.99	2.62
Summer 94	2.68	1.06	1.62	0.58	0.33	0.97	2.52
Autumn 94	2.47	n.a.	n.a.	n.a.	n.a.	0.91	n.a.

Source: *Labour Force Survey* (various).

Table 5
ILO unemployed non-claimants, men & women, GB, not seasonally-adjusted (millions)

Year	Men 000s	Men % seeking part-time work	Women 000s	Women % seeking part-time work	Men & women 000s	Men & women % seeking part-time work
1971	80	n.a.	230	n.a.	310	n.a.
1975	80	n.a.	320	n.a.	400	n.a.
1977	80	n.a.	340	n.a.	420	n.a.
1979	80	n.a.	200	n.a.	300	n.a.
Spring 81	130	n.a.	270	n.a.	400	n.a.
Spring 83	220	n.a.	540	n.a.	820	n.a.
Spring 84	250	n.a.	620	n.a.	870	n.a.
Spring 84	230	10.9	640	44.4	870	35.5
Spring 85	230	21.7	600	64.2	840	51.9
Spring 86	230	23.9	580	63.1	810	52.0
Spring 87	250	20.0	590	60.3	840	48.6
Spring 88	260	15.4	520	65.0	770	49.1
Spring 89	320	16.9	530	57.4	850	42.0
Spring 90	330	16.4	530	58.9	860	42.6
Spring 91	340	15.6	540	56.1	890	40.0
Spring 92	390	10.3	500	53.8	890	35.1
Summer 92	450	11.3	550	45.5	1010	29.9
Autumn 92	430	12.6	550	51.1	980	34.4
Winter 92/3	460	12.6	540	51.3	990	33.9
Spring 1992	430	11.6	510	53.5	950	34.1
Summer 1993	500	n.a.	580	n.a.	1080	n.a.
Autumn 93	474	n.a.	563	n.a.	1037	n.a.
Winter 93/4	457	n.a.	534	n.a.	991	n.a.
Spring 94	436	n.a.	527	n.a.	964	n.a.
Summer 94	527	n.a.	536	n.a.	1063	n.a.

Source: *Employment Gazette* (various). The series on 'unregistered unemployed' for 1971-81 can be found in *Gazette* (June 1983).

The high degree of agreement between ILO and claimant unemployment in total follows from the fact that, given the core of ILO unemployed claimants common to both measures, the number of ILO unemployed non-claimants roughly equals those claimants not ILO unemployed. However, except arithmetically, these two groups do not offset one another in any real sense — as they comprise very different populations. In fact, the relationship between the two, we shall argue here, is, to a large extent, additive.

ILO unemployed non-claimants

This group comprises, according to the ED, 'those people who are not entitled to claim certain unemployment benefits in their own right and also those who may not wish or consider it worthwhile to claim'.

In the past, women constituted the overwhelming majority of this group, for several reasons: low earnings (below the National Insurance threshold, currently £57 per week) preclude entitlement to UB as does opting to make reduced rate contributions; an inadequate contribution record, perhaps because having only recently returned to the labour force, rules out a successful claim for UB; or women may find themselves unable to claim means-tested IS (following exhaustion of UB due to long-duration unemployment or UB disqualification due to 'voluntary' unemployment), because their partner is either working or already claiming benefit.

However, recently, men have increased rapidly amongst ILO unemployed non-claimants — almost to the point of parity with women. This may reflect the adverse effect on men's ability to claim means-tested IS of increased employment by female spouses. Also, male self-employment fell by 300,000 during the recession; ineligible for UB, such men may also be ineligible for means-tested IS on account of the £8,000 personal capital rule or the employment of their spouses. ILO unemployed non-claimants also include the unemployed 16 & 17 year-olds discussed earlier.

ILO unemployed non-claimants, after doubling with the rise of mass unemployment in the early 1980s, have shown a small trend increase since 1984 — but with no cyclical sensitivity. Nevertheless, all 1.08 million ILO unemployed non-claimants ought to be counted as unemployed — their exclusion from the claimant count being solely for administrative reasons.

Claimants not-ILO unemployed

How should the 1 million unemployed claimants who are not considered ILO unemployed (see Table 4) — because either in employment or inactive according to the ILO definition — be treated?

Employed claimants

This group, whose very existence may come as a surprise to many, comprises claimants who are regarded as employed, according to the ILO guidelines, because they work more than 1 hour in the reference week. 330,000 claimants were in this position in summer 1993 — a doubling in numbers (see Table 6).

The ED, in its annual analysis of these figures, is always at pains to stress that this series 'is not necessarily an indication of activity

Table 6
Claimants in employment, GB, not seasonally-adjusted (000s)

	Men	*Women*	*Men & women*
Spring 1983	90	70	160
Spring 1984	110	60	170
Spring 1985	110	80	190
Spring 1986	120	70	190
Spring 1987	120	60	180
Spring 1988	130	60	190
Spring 1989	140	70	210
Spring 1990	140	50	190
Spring 1991	200	60	260
Spring 1992	230	90	320
Summer 1992	200	80	280
Autumn 1992	260	80	350
Winter 92/3	270	90	360
Spring 1993	290	90	380
Summer 1993	250	80	330
Autumn 1993	273	83	356
Winter 93/4	275	84	359
Spring 1994	289	77	367
Summer 1994	255	76	332

Source: *Employment Gazette* (various) since 1983, with virtually all of the increase occurring amongst men, though with little evidence of cyclicality.

in the "black" economy, since in some circumstances people can legitimately claim unemployment-related benefits while they also have relatively low earnings from part-time work' (*Employment Gazette*, October 1993, p.462). Briefly, those on UB can earn up to £57 a week and still claim benefit except for days where more than £2 is earned; on IS, up to 16 hours a week paid employment can be worked, though, beyond a £5 disregard, benefit is reduced £ for £ of net earnings. Note that a few of these employed claimants 'will have become unemployed or started a job part way through the reference week' (*Employment Gazette*, October 1985, p.462).

Increasing numbers of employed claimants are indicative of a growing army of men combining low part-time, casual earnings with unemployment-related benefits in order to survive. This must reflect the emergence of mass unemployment and the decline in male employment opportunities in the 1980s. To quote the *Employment Gazette* (October 1993, p.462): 'Some of the increase in "claimant employment" in recent years may be explained by changes in the economic cycle. In a recessionary situation characterised by continually rising unemployment and diminishing job prospects, one may see an increase in "claimant employment" as more unemployed people accept the sort of part-time jobs which, because they only generate low earnings, do not preclude job-holders from also claiming benefits'.

Should 'employed claimants' be counted amongst the unemployed? The answer must surely be 'yes'. Given the restrictions on the amount that can be earned whilst still receiving benefit, 'employed claimants' are not earning very much nor are many hours being worked. The 'claimant employed' must certainly be considered severely underemployed (whether measured in terms of income or hours worked) — and, thus, to a very large degree, unemployed as well.

Claimants not ILO unemployed because inactive

And how should we treat those claimants not considered ILO-unemployed because 'inactive' — either because they were not seeking work or because they were not available: in total numbering 660,000 (470,000 men and 190,000 women) in summer 1993. That such large numbers of claimants exhibiting these characteristics should exist at all is somewhat surprising, given: (i) that 'availability' and, since 1988, 'actively seeking' are basic conditions for receiving unemployment-related benefits — with both conditions having been more rigorously applied in recent years; and (ii) the unceasing drive against benefit fraud. Indeed, such is the vigour with which the benefit regime is applied that it might be suggested all 'inactive' claimants should be treated as unemployed.

However, amongst 'inactive' claimants, the *Labour Force Survey* finds large numbers declaring they do not wish to work (260,000 in spring 1993); these cannot be treated as involuntarily unemployed. The principal reasons given for not looking are: amongst men — long-term sickness/disablement and retirement, in which case they should be transferred to alternative benefits, and, amongst women — looking after family/home. Other claimants giving 'long-term sickness/disablement' as their reason for 'inactivity' (roughly 30,000) should be on alternative benefits and also cannot be treated as unemployed.

However, should some of the remaining 'inactive' claimants be treated as unemployed? It should be noted that 'inactive' claimants are highly cyclical (see Table 4) — strongly suggesting *a priori* that they might be included amongst the (cyclical) unemployed. One explanation is that the intensity of job search is linked to the economic cycle — increases in 'inactivity' reflecting 'discouragement'. The *Labour Force Survey* publishes a series of those ILO 'inactives' who are 'discouraged' — defined as 'those who

Table 7
'Discouraged' workers; GB, not seasonally-adjusted, thousands

| | Discouraged workers* | | |
	Total	Men	Women
Spring 84	225	119	106
Spring 85	224	130	94
Spring 86	223	145	78
Spring 87	148	89	59
Spring 88	115	74	42
Spring 89	107	47	29
Spring 90	77	47	30
Spring 91	77	47	30
Spring 92	151 (122)	79 (65)	72 (57)
Summer 92	157 (124)	86 (70)	71 (54)
Autumn 92	176 (139)	97 (79)	79 (60)
Winter 92/3	188 (147)	98 (78)	90 (69)
Spring 93	178 (133)	100 (77)	78 (55)
Summer 93	181 (141)	105 (82)	76 (60)
Autumn 93	184 (137)	107 (77)	77 (61)
Winter 93/4	191 (139)	111 (81)	80 (58)
Spring 94	169 (122)	99 (73)	69 (49)
Summer 94	170 (128)	98 (75)	72 (52)

Source: *Labour Force Survey* (various).
*Men and women aged 16+ (data in brackets are for men aged 16-64 and women aged 16-59).

would like work but have not looked in the past 4 weeks as they believe there are no jobs available' (see Table 7) — some of whom are claimants and others not. 'Discouraged' workers would be included by most economists amongst the unemployed.

Excluding from the total of 'inactive' claimants those who do not wish to work, the long-term sick/disabled and 'discouraged' workers, there remain between 250,000 and 300,000 claimants over whom there hangs a question mark as to whether or not they should be included amongst the unemployed. Reasons given for failing to look for a job during the previous week include: looking after family/home, temporarily sick, on holiday, awaiting results of job application, waiting to start job already obtained, studying, not yet started looking. For each of these reasons, some sort of argument could be made for classifying the person involved as unemployed rather than 'inactive'. For example, claimants who fail to engage in job search because temporarily sick ought surely to be treated as unemployed since they are only briefly outside the labour market — even though they ought properly to be on sickness benefit. A similar argument holds for those claimants who have not yet started looking for work. Those awaiting the results of a job application or waiting to start a job already obtained, even if not available, might also be classed as unemployed. In the case of claimants on holiday, benefit regulations permit claimants to take a holiday, so long as they remain 'available' even if, for obvious reasons, they cannot be engaged in active job search; taking a holiday should surely not disqualify a claimant from being counted as unemployed. Even claimants who are looking after family/home, thereby precluding job search, cannot necessarily be regarded as putting themselves permanently beyond the job market — since absence may be temporary (due to illness in the family or the collapse of existing care arrangements) or may reflect 'discouragement'. Thus, a high proportion of ILO 'inactive' claimants ought surely to be counted as unemployed — always bearing in mind that all claimants are satisfying those administering the benefit regime as to their 'capability, availability and active search' for work.

Neither ILO nor claimant unemployed

Some unemployed people in receipt of benefit are not required to 'sign on' (hence, excluded from the claimant count) and, since they are not engaged in active job search, are also not ILO unemployed. An obvious group are men aged 60 and over in receipt of IS or NI credits who are no longer required to 'sign on'. Some of these, if they still express a desire to work, may be included amongst the 'discouraged' workers already discussed. But, many of them, demoralised by the lack of employment prospects, have probably given up wanting and looking for work (i.e. they have accepted involuntary premature retirement). They should, none the less, be treated as unemployed. Around 200,000 men aged 60 and over were affected by dispensing with the need to 'sign on' in the early 1980s.

Alternative unemployment measure

Our alternative unemployment measure (see Table 8) starts with ILO unemployment (ILO unemployed claimants plus ILO unemployed non-claimants), and adds in claimant employed plus 'discouraged' workers and those on government work-related training programmes. We then sum together: 'inactive' claimants (having subtracted 'those who do not wish to work' as well as 'long-term sick/disabled') together with men aged 60 and over not 'signing-on' and take an admittedly arbitrary figure of 50% as an estimate of those unemployed.

Unemployment in summer 1993, measured in this way, appears closer to the Unemployment Unit's total of 4 million than to the official claimant count of under 3 million.

Table 8
An alternative unemployment measure: summer 1993, not seasonally-adjusted, millions

	Total	Men	Women
Claimant unemployed (UK)	2.81	2.14	0.67
ILO unemployed claimants (GB)	1.82	1.42	0.39
+ ILO unemployed non-claimants (GB)	1.08	0.50	0.58
+ claimants: in employment (GB)	0.33	0.25	0.08
+ 'discouraged' workers of working-age (incl claimants) (GB)	0.141	0.082	0.06
+ government work-related training programmes (GB)	0.306	0.200	0.106
Claimants: other 'inactive' less claimant 'discouraged'(GB)	0.590	0.400	0.190
Less 'would not like work' and 'long-term sick/disabled'	-0.300	-0.200*	-0.100*
= *Other 'inactive'/? unemployed claimants (GB)	0.290	0.200	0.090
*Men aged 60 and over not 'signing on'	0.200	0.200	0.0
+ 50% of *categories	0.245	0.200	0.045
Total alternative unemployment (GB)	3.922	2.652	1.261
Total alternative unemployment (UK)	4.07	2.750	1.316

Source: *Labour Force Survey.*

Disappearing men

Further support for the view that claimant unemployment understates the true size of the problem by at least 1 million can be gained from the large increase in male 'inactivity' between 1979-93: the number of men of working-age classified as neither employed nor unemployed rose by 1.145 million between 1979-93. Table 9 contains the details.

During cyclical down-turns, the fall in male employment exceeds the rise in ILO unemployment — and large numbers of men 'disappear' into inactivity. During the early 1990s recession, for example, male employment declined by 1.3 million, whilst ILO unemployment rose by just 836,000; taking into account the addition to the male working-age population of 113,000, a total of 579,000 men 'disappeared' from the statistician's gaze. Similarly, during cyclical recoveries (e.g. the Lawson boom of the late 1980s), increases in employment exceed declines in ILO unemployment — as men are drawn from 'inactivity'. Both phenomena point to the existence of a substantial penumbra of male labour reserves around male unemployment as officially measured.

Taking longer periods of time, large numbers of men have 'disappeared' into 'inactivity', either comparing peaks in cyclical activity (1979-90) or taking the period of Conservative rule from 1979 to 1993. Comparing 1979-93, reductions in male employment (-1.18 million) roughly equal increases in ILO unemployment (+1.147 million) leaving

Table 9
Disappearing men: changes in male employment, unemployment and population of working-age, since 1979, GB, seasonally-adjusted, 000s

Year	Employment	Change	Unemployment	Change	Workforce	Change	Population of working age	Participation change
1979	14824		774		15598		109	
1980							81	
1981	14174	-650	1570	796	15744	146	85	-29
1982							69	
1983	13642	-532	1825	255	15470	-274	134	-477
1984	13790	148	1848	23	15639	169	141	30
1985	13931	141	1798	-50	15730	91	101	-10
1986	13886	-45	1796	-2	15682	-48	88	-135
1987	14032	146	1724	-72	15756	74	100	-26
1988	14492	460	1401	-323	15893	137	77	60
1989	14858	366	1146	-255	16004	111	70	41
1990	14496	88	1085	-61	16031	27	56	-29
1991	14500	-446	1424	339	15924	-107	36	-143
1992	13983	-517	1775	351	15758	-166	37	-203
1993	13644	-339	1921	146	15564	-194	40	-233
1979-90		+122		+311		+433	+1002	-566
1979-93		-1180		+1147		-34	+1115	-1145

Source: Labour Force Surveys as reported in *Economic Trends*, October 1993, p.44.

Notes:
Estimates of the male working-age population derived by applying constant 1985 age-specific participation rates to the changing population age profile over time (*Employment Gazette*, April 1992, 173-183).

Table 10
Invalidity benefit: number of claimants (thousands), 1971-94

Year	Men Total	Men of working age 16-64	Women Total	Women of working age 16-60	Men & women Total	Men & women of working age
1971/2	334	322	81	79	415	401
1972/3	355	341	81	78	436	419
1973/4	366	349	78	75	444	424
1974/5	373	352	79	76	452	428
1975/6	400	382	79	76	479	458
1976/7	422	397	84	81	506	478
1977/8	462	430	97	93	559	523
1978/9	505	467	107	102	612	569
1979/80	506	459	109	104	615	563
1980/1	517	470	116	111	633	581
1981/2	553	503	130	123	683	626
1982/3	593	538	144	137	737	675
1983/4	638	579	159	150	797	729
1984/5	673	601	177	165	850	766
1985/6	706	619	193	179	899	798
1986/7	754	644	214	197	968	841
1987/8	808	678	240	220	1048	898
1988/9	860	709	266	243	1126	952
1989/90	917	740	293	264	1210	1004
1990/1	976	775	330	293	1306	1068
1991/2	1063	844	376	331	1439	1175
1992/3	1156	927	424	371	1580	1298
1993/4					1585	
1994/5					1680	

Source: *Social Security Statistics* (various) and *Government's expenditure plans: social security* (Cm 2213)., p.45.

the male work-force roughly constant; however, expansionary demographic factors caused the male working-age population to rise by 1.115 million. Thus, male 'inactivity' rose by 1.145 million.

Some of these men 'disappeared' into inactivity as a result of increased participation in tertiary education and voluntary early retirement. But, for the great majority, increased 'inactivity' was involuntary — reflecting the deterioration in male employment opportunities as well as the opportunity for switching into invalidity benefit.

Invalidity benefit

The rapid increase in the number of claimants in receipt of invalidity benefit — 1 million since 1979 (see Table 10) — helps to explain how some of the hugely increased numbers of 'inactive' males were able to support themselves as well as providing further evidence for the existence of 1 million missing unemployed.

Invalidity Benefit (IVB) is payable to those who remain 'incapable of work' after they have exhausted their 28 week entitlement to Statutory Sick Pay (SSP) and Sickness Benefit (SB). It is payable at a higher rate than the two unemployment-related benefits (UB, IS) and is not currently taxable, unlike the State Retirement Pension — which explains why large numbers choose to remain on IVB and defer entitlement to their pension. Incapacity Benefit, which replaces Invalidity Benefit and Sickness Benefit from April 1995, will be taxable.

Four factors suggest that IVB has been used as an alternative to unemployment-related benefits: (i) the higher level of payment; (ii) the fact that the 1 million increase in IVB claimants since 1979 follows a decade (of much lower unemployment levels) when the number of IVB claimants increased by just 200,000 (50%); (iii) the numbers of claimants of Industrial Injury Benefit has remained virtually constant at around 200,000 since 1979; (iv) performance targets set the Employment Service to reduce the number on the count — by, amongst other things, transferring people on to alternative (non-unemployment-related) benefits. Recent discussion suggests some doctors have taken 'employability' into account in assessing 'incapacity'.

Additional evidence on unemployment

Additional evidence from the *Labour Force Survey* confirms that the claimant count understates the true level of involuntary unemployment by a considerable amount (see Table 11). Everyone not employed or unemployed and, hence, classified 'inactive' is asked in the *LFS* whether they would like a job if one were available. This reveals (in addition to almost 3 million ILO unemployed) some 2 million or more people who would like paid employment: more than 0.5 million men and roughly 1.5 million women. This group sub-divides further according to the strength of labour market attachment. First, a million people in the 1980s (two-thirds of whom were women) — falling to 800,000 in 1992 — who, though they had not engaged in job search, were available for work (results of *LFS* tabulation reported in Unemployment Unit, *Working Brief*). Thus, relaxing the job search criterion for ILO unemployment whilst retaining the availability condition, yields a total unsatisfied demand for work in the region of 4 million. One justification for doing so is to be found in the qualification appended to the ILO unemployment definition: 'In situations . . . *where labour absorption is at the time inadequate . . .* the standard definition of unemployment . . . may be applied by relaxing the criterion of seeking work.' (Resolution I of the 13th International Conference of Labour Statisticians). If both 'search' and 'availability' criteria are relaxed, there are a further 1 million persons who would also like paid employment

— though their labour market attachment is considerably weaker.

The main characteristics of these two groups are fairly similar: married and non-married women carers looking after the family/home and amongst men: 'discouraged' workers, (early, possibly involuntary) retirees and long-term sick/disabled. Whilst undoubtedly part of the economy's labour reserve, many such people could only take paid employment if, for example, greater support could be given to those caring for dependent relatives.

Conclusions on claimant count

The claimant count clearly understates the true level of unemployment by a wide margin. Nor is claimant unemployment a very sensitive indicator of changing labour market conditions. For one thing, it is far from clear that movements in an item which is a sub-set of a larger variable are necessarily an accurate guide to movements in the latter. Moreover, the claimant count is necessarily sensitive to administrative action affecting inflows and outflows. Thus, the 602,000 decline in claimant unemployment since early 1993 may reflect the increased success of the Employment Service at placing people from the count into jobs — possibly at the expense of new entrants and the 'inactive' — rather than a dramatic improvement in underlying labour market conditions.

Table 11
Alternative measure of labour reserve: GB, seasonally-adjusted, thousands

	ILO unemployed	Inactive, want work, available in next two weeks, not engaged in job search in past 4 weeks			Inactive, want work, not free to start in next two weeks, whether or not engaged in job search in past 4 weeks		
	Total	Total	Men	Women	Total	Men	Women
Spring 1984	3105	1250	400	850	954	n.a.	n.a.
Spring 1985	2980	1204	378	826	1015	n.a.	n.a.
Spring 1986	2981	1316	454	862	1003	n.a.	n.a.
Spring 1987	2890	1180	380	800	796	284	512
Spring 1988	2385	1130	367	763	848	294	554
Spring 1989	1983	1087	360	727	1003	340	663
Spring 1990	1871	1024	330	694	n.a.	n.a.	n.a.
Spring 1991	2301	1028	332	696	n.a.	n.a.	n.a.
Spring 1992	2649	770	206	564	944	n.a.	n.a.
Summer 1992	2758	771	216	555	944	n.a.	n.a.
Autumn 1992	2837	760	218	541	n.a.	n.a.	n.a.
Winter 93/94	2729	1000	400	600	1300	500	807
Summer 1994	2637	900	400	600	1300	500	800

Source: Unemployment Unit, *Unemployment Bulletin* and *Working Brief* (various) and Employment Department, *Gazette.*

CHAPTER THREE

Measuring Employment in Britain

*Some problems of meaning and reliability
in the official series*

John Hughes

Over the years a false picture of employment in Britain has all too
often been created by presentation of official statistics. The
weaknesses and manipulation involved takes many forms. We are
familiar with the idea that the unemployment data have been
changed time and again, primarily to diminish the published totals.
But the cumulative possibilities of building a false consciousness
about employment have also been apparent. There have also been
problems of the reliability of published data, which are more severe
for employment series than for unemployment; on occasion,
officialdom having created hundreds of thousands of jobs through
processes of dubious estimation has had (discreetly and quietly, of
course) to wipe them out in 'revised' series.

The problems are not ones involving great technical
sophistication. So what is attempted here is to outline some of the
main types of pollution of the employment data that, from past
experience, have confused the underlying reality. After that, there
is a closer look at recent failings in the handling of employment
measurement in the 1990s (partly necessary as officialdom writes
itself references about the 'improvement' of methods of
measurement at the very moment it is worsening the coverage).
There are some outline figures over the last fifteen years which may
clear up some aspects of Britain's track record.

One set of confusions arises because Government, seeking to
show employment 'creation', puts quite different things together in
aggregate series. This is particularly important in relation to
part-time as against full-time employment. It also appears as a result
of redefining the 'workforce' to include in it groups of people not
previously counted.

Let us take up the issues involved:

(i) What weight for part-time employees?

A persistent feature of the economy over the last decade and a half is the long term decline in the total numbers of employees in full-time work, and an expansion in the number of part-timers. Obviously, if we are seeking to understand what is happening to labour inputs (and also labour incomes) over a period of time, we have to recognise that a full-time employee in employment does not represent the same unit of work as a part-time one. Series which simply measure total numbers of both may give a very misleading impression.

This can be allowed for if we can estimate how many part-timers may represent total hours of employment equivalent to a full-time worker; then comparisons over time can be made in terms of 'full-time equivalence'. In the past, the New Earnings Survey analysis of hours worked pointed to two part-time employees as being equivalent in hours worked to one full-timer. But NES coverage of part-time work is far from complete, as it is based on a sample of National Insurance numbers; part-timers earning less than the National Insurance threshold are excluded (and these might well be expected to work fewer hours).

However, more recently, detailed analysis of hours of work using a differently based survey, the Labour Force Survey, has provided a new source of data relating to part-time hours. The Labour Force Survey for 1991, for which detailed hours analysis has been published (see especially, *Employment Gazette*, November 1992) relates to an estimated 5.1 million part-time employees. (The 1993 NES data on part-time hours relates by contrast to some 4 million). The Official Department of Employment figures for 1991 estimate a total of some 5.8 million part-time employees in employment in Britain. Clearly, the LFS can claim to be surveying the great majority of these.

The Labour Force Survey data gives the following overall figures of average weekly hours actually worked:

Male Employees	Full-Time	45.3 hours
	Part-Time	15.7 hours
Female Employees	Full-Time	40.3 hours
	Part-Time	17.0 hours

(Data relates to 1991).

From these figures the ratios that emerge are significantly different from 2:1 of the New Earnings Survey. For males, average part-time hours are only 35% of the hours of full-time workers; for female employees, average part-time hours are 42% of full-time hours. It is these ratios that it would seem most appropriate to use in constructing overall estimates of full-time equivalent employment. Taken together these figures give close to a 5:2 ratio for full-time equivalence, but it is important to recognise the different ratios now apparent for male and for female employees.

It is not difficult to illustrate the different perception of employment trends that emerge once this question of 'weighting' part-time work is taken into account. Table 1 gives figures for employees in employment in Great Britain for mid-1994, and for exactly ten years earlier (on both occasions these are dates shortly after the economy had emerged from a cyclical trough in employment):

Table 1
GB Employees in Employment; June 1984 and June 1994 (in thousands)

	Total	Full-time employees	Part-time Actual	Part-time As FT equiv.	Total in full-time equiv.
June 84	20,741	16,063	4,679	1,910	17,973
June 94	20,908	14,968	5,940	2,416	17,384
Change	+167	-1,095	+1,261	+506	-589

Sources: *Employment Gazette,* Jan. 1995 and Historical Supplement (October 94). For explanation of full-time equivalence, see text.

The crude employment total suggests a gain in employees in employment in June 1994 as compared with June 1984 of 167 thousand. But this emerges from a decline in full-time employment of over one million, and an offsetting rise in part-time employment of just over one and a quarter million. When part-time employment is measured in full-time equivalents (FTEs), its rise is reduced to 506 thousand (FTEs). In the final column we have the total restated as full-time equivalents throughout; it shows a decline over the period of nearly 600 thousand. This is the best available measure of the weighted employment trend over the period, and affords a very different picture to that derived from the crude total.

If we carried out a similar exercise (using the same sources and methods) comparing June 1994 with fifteen years earlier (i.e mid 1979) as the Conservative Government came into office, we would find that even the crude total of employees in employment cannot conceal the fall in employees in employment. The June 1979 figure was 22,638,000, nearly one and three-quarters of a million higher than in 1994. But the weighted 'full-time equivalent' figure for 1979 is even more damning; it is just under 19.9 million, or two and a half million full-time equivalents higher than in 1994.

(ii) Double-counting

Part-time employment also means that the published figures of employment are inflated by double-counting. The normal employment data are based on returns from employers, so that people with two — or more — jobs are counted separately by each employer, and will be double-counted in the employment total. No allowance for this is made when the employment figures are published; but not only is the total at any one time exaggerated. If more people in the labour force are holding two jobs than in earlier years, this will distort the trend in published employment. As full-time jobs decline in number and part-time employment is increasing, this is exactly what takes place.

It is possible to track this phenomenon through the quarterly Labour Force Survey (though that survey involves problems of reliability, due to its modest sample size and method of data collection). The latest figures, for Summer 1994, show 981,000 people who were employees in their 'first' job, stating that they had a second job (an estimated 738 thousand of these were as employees, but 242 thousand were recorded as 'self-employed'). In all (including self-employed people who had multiple jobs) there was a total of 1.17 million 'second jobs'. Interestingly, an additional 133,000 second jobs were held as employees compared with summer 1993. Now, the total employment in Britain (employees in employment) for June 1994 was published — as we saw in Table 1 set out earlier — as 20,908,000. The published figure for June 1993 was 21,011,000. On the crude figures, that looks like a decline in employees in employment compared with a year earlier of some 100,000. But if we take into account the 133,000 or so increase in second jobs, the employment decline as it affected people must have been nearer a quarter of a million between mid 1993 and mid 1994.

Thus the treatment of part-time employees in employment in the official statistics for employment in Great Britain greatly exaggerates and distorts its scale and significance. Given this over-emphasis on the rising levels of part-time work, a statistic from the 1991 Labour Force Survey from which a detailed analysis of hours worked was derived (see *Employment Gazette*, November 1992), is worth noting. Of the total hours worked by all employees in 1991, 89% were accounted for by full-time work, only 11% by part-time work.

(iii) Job creation by re-defining the 'work-force'

The clearest example of 'creating' employment by inventing a new category of 'workers' is that for 'work related government training programmes'. This was introduced by the Government in the late 1980s (official notes introducing the series are to be found in the August 1988 *Employment Gazette*). The numbers in this new category, for the United Kingdom, had risen to around 450,000 by 1989. This appeared, consequently, as an increase of that scale in the 'workforce in employment' as compared with the early 1980s when no such training is recorded. The official 'explanation' for the series is highly revealing. The new category contains participants in 'work-based' training without contracts of employment (those with contracts had already — quite properly — been counted as employees in employment). It seems an odd defining characteristic of a 'worker' that there is no contract of employment. All those in the category are treated as part-time, since 'part of their time is spent on training activity'; nevertheless, each appears as a whole unit of employment in the aggregated figures. The August 1988 official notes actually admit the 'smallness of the contribution of scheme participants to output', although this was, of course, the excuse for including them in the first place. Finally, which is highly ironic from a Government that has repudiated so many ILO standards protecting workers' conditions, it is suggested that the new category was 'in line' with ILO suggestions.

This invention of a new category not only appeared to show higher employment. It has the effect of slightly reducing the officially published rate of unemployment, since this is calculated in relation to the 'total workforce', now swollen by this non-contractual 'small contribution' work-related category.

(iv) Employment creation by altering the basis of estimation

A recent good example of this kind of statistical initiative is to be found in the case of the estimates of the number of 'self-employed'. In a difficult period for the government in 1993/94 when, for all the talk of 'green shoots' of recovery, the employment totals were falling, the official estimates for the number of self-employed were subjected to 'an upward revision of 187,000 at December 1993'. This arose from a decision to base estimates solely on the Labour Force Survey. That survey is based on only one in 350 households. Only 80% of the selected households respond. Attempts are made to interview each household member aged 16 and over, as to their economic activity, but one-third of 'respondents' are actually answered for by another adult member of the household. On the basis of respondents' 'self-assessment', and on 'grossing up' from this modest sample, the estimates of self-employed numbers are derived.

For a number of years until the latest change of statistical base, estimates of the number of self-employed have been 'benchmarked' on the 1981 Census of Population. The Census is not a sample survey but a 100% return; the figure of the number of self-employed revealed by the 1981 Census has been used as the most reliable source for 1981, rather than the relatively small (60,000 households) Labour Force Survey. The relative or 'trend' movements in the self-employed shown by successive Labour Force Surveys have been used to make updated estimates since the 1981 Census. One would have thought that this approach would have been vindicated when the 1991 Census of Population became available. The 1991 Census showed for April 1991 a total of 3,078,000 self-employed; the estimates built up since the 1981 Census showed 3,066,000 for June 1991. Since the recession in the labour market was developing, it would seem that the system of estimation had proved extremely reliable.

And yet the decision has been made — and implemented in the new estimates — to abandon the connection with the Census of Population, and only use the Labour Force Survey estimates. This means that the 100% coverage of the Census is disregarded, and the LFS survey — which is smaller in scale than the New Earnings Survey, and constitutes less than 1% of households — is preferred. The sense of special pleading on this is very evident in the pages of the May 1994 *Employment Gazette* which deals with this (pages 168-169). For instance, the LFS is referred to as a 'very large survey' at this point, whereas earlier it is accurately stated that it is a survey of '60,000 households each quarter'. P.169 pleads that it is 'designed to provide reliable and consistent information on the employment characteristics of the whole population'. Yet, a survey that is so small in relation to the total number of private households must be subject to sampling errors and problems of reliability.[1]

The special pleading even extends to an attempt to challenge the reliability of the Census of Population: 'the Census relies purely on people classifying themselves as self-employed, whereas the LFS *has the advantage that this self-classification is aided by trained interviewers*'. (My emphasis.)

This is a very unusual degree of special pleading. The *Gazette* apologist goes on to argue (p.168): 'it is likely that in the Census some people ignored small amounts of own-account work', which should have led to their being counted as self-employed. If this is a telling argument, it tells against the new change in basis; for it would only be 'small amounts' that would be ignored, rather than anything approaching full-time self-employment. But the Census of Population added its own 10% sample (vastly bigger than that of the LFS) in which the Census returns were subjected to additional validation checks. The self-employed estimates resulting from that additional process of specialist validation was not higher than the 100% Census, but lower (2,935,000); this, the *Employment Gazette* argues, was partly for technical reasons (e.g. owner-managers of limited companies are excluded). But the significant point is that it offers no support for the latest official attempt to reach out for the highest figure of self-employment available, even if that means repudiating the Census of Population and its evidently greater reliability.

It has, however, given the Government an upward revision of self-employed numbers which, by December 1993, were 187,000 higher than they would have been if the previous system of 'benchmarking' on the Census of Population had continued. (The inflation of the self-employed figures has been carried back through to June 1971). The LFS figures are to be used throughout in total disregard of the markedly different figures coming from successive Censuses of Population. It is, nevertheless, a petty and unconvincing exercise in statistical job creation. After all, as has previously been noted, the only argument advanced for preferring the LFS figures is that 'some people' might 'ignore small amounts of own account work'. The 187,000 inflation of the figure at best represents 'small amounts' of work. But it does represent a large and unworthy amount of statistical juggling.

(v) Major weaknesses in estimates of employees in employment

One might have thought that official data on the number of employees would be more reliably based, since there are periodic Censuses of Employment collected from employers. (Though as we have seen, this does not eliminate double-counting of those holding more than one job.) But as an 'economy' measure, the government in the 1980s reduced these to a Census only every three years (in 1981, 1984, and 1987), and this was only restored to a two year interval in 1989. There are also very lengthy delays in publishing these Employment Censuses. Thus, the results of the 1987 Census were only published in Autumn 1989, so that official data on employees in employment had been based on estimates for five whole years. The September 1989 Census results were only published in April 1991, so estimation had been the order of the day prior to that publication, for three and a half years. During those long periods of estimation, large and significant errors occurred, with a persistent tendency to exaggerate the numbers in employment.

This led to attempts to improve estimation, in the light of the 1989 Census with a redesigned 'panel' of respondent firms. But early in 1994 it was announced that yet another 'panel' of firms had been designed for purposes of estimation in the light of the 1991 Census of Employment. The new panel system was also ushered in with an upward revision to the previous calculations as to employees in employment since the 1991 Census. For December 1993, the estimated total has been increased by 149,000. This seems a large revision to come out of a redesigned panel, so it is worth examining closely whether 'change' actually does mean 'improvement' in coverage and reliability. It is also interesting to notice that, somewhat carelessly, the upward revision of employee in employment estimates is restricted to Great Britain alone. Somewhat surprisingly, no revision was made to the Northern Ireland figures.

The May 1994 *Employment Gazette* set out in detail why revisions in the 'panel' had been felt necessary. The 1991 Census had shown a case for 're-weighting' the panel of workplaces, both in terms of changing industrial composition (from production industries into services) and changing workplace size (with a shift from medium sized workplaces towards smaller ones). This may well have been reflecting the major recession of the early 1990s, which affected production industries more than service ones, and which contracted employment more generally. Whether this fits the likely pattern of recovery may be less sure. It still seems surprising that the re-weighting should have led so swiftly to a considerable upward adjustment in the estimated employment totals, since we are told that the previous 'panel' of respondents had 'performed well' in tracking changes in employment between the Census dates of 1989 and 1991.

In practice, there must be serious doubts as to the adequacy of the new 'panel' from which current employment estimates are derived. This is particularly due to a retreat from the coverage required, in deference to attacks on the 'burden of form-filling', and as a result of continuing advocacy of deregulation; so we read,

> 'The panel must be of limited size to avoid unacceptable form-filling burdens on employers, and has been kept at 30,000 workplaces for many years' (*Gazette*, May 1994, p.167)

Bravo! And, therefore, if there is a shift to smaller workplaces in the re-weighted panel, the coverage is likely to be reduced. And this is what happens in practice. The only tangible gain is in services where the proportion of 'workplaces' covered goes up from a grossly inadequate 2% to a still quite inadequate 3%. In production industries the proportion comes down from 7% to 5%. The proportion of employees covered is lower in the new '1991 panel' than in the old '1989 panel' in both sectors: it falls in services from 21% to 19%, and in production from 49% to 44%. If this is reform and improvement, we need to redefine our terms. Moreover, as the number of employees has itself been falling, the fall in total number covered by the sample workplaces has fallen even more distinctly. The May 1994 *Employment Gazette* (page 167) states that 4,705,000 employees were covered by the 1989 panel, but the figure for coverage by the new 1991 panel is only 3,846,000, a reduction of 18%.

Past experience of the performance of official estimates between Censuses of Employment has shown a very considerable tendency to overestimate the upswing, and indeed to overestimate in general. For instance:

i) The Censuses of Employment showed a rise of just over 450 thousand in employees in employment from September 1984 to September 1987. The official estimate had been over 300,000 higher.

ii) The estimates of growth in employees in employment between the 1987 and 1989 Censuses turned out to be over 125,000 too high.

iii) While the boom progressed between September 1989 and September 1990, official estimates were for an increase in employees in employment of 395,000. But later, when it was clear the cycle had turned, the official estimates for those dates were cut back to only 101,000. We cannot, however, say which estimate was 'right', though the latter figure was probably more reliable. It is the difference (of nearly 300,000) in official estimates for the same period that is worth noting.

In the light of past failings, and with a 'panel' with inadequate coverage, it seemed that there might be merit in looking at some of the details of officially recorded changes in employment by industry or service sector (Table 1.4. of the *Employment Gazette*) for 1993, using the same May 1994 issue. The various sectors were examined to see if major increases in employment were being recorded on any scale.

A bizarre conclusion emerged. Service sectors with a major employment increase were the 'not elsewhere specified' (n.e.s.) parts of the finance sector and of retail distribution. The employment increases recorded in these 'n.e.s.' sectors were disproportionately high by comparison with the main identified constituents of the sectors concerned. If there has been an employment recovery it is 'not elsewhere specified'!

Example: finance sector estimates

Within the 'banking, finance, and insurance' sector is a residual category, 'business services not elsewhere specified (n.e.s.)'. This sector, in December 1992, was estimated to employ 450 thousand of the 2,600,000 in the 'banking, etc.' sector. Yet this sector (according to Table 1.4 of the *Gazette*), which accounted for only 17% of employment in its sector, is officially estimated to have accounted for 80% of the sector's employment increase. According to the May 1994 *Gazette*, this 'Business Services n.e.s.' raised its employment by a phenomenal 77 thousand — a 17% increase — in the year from December 1992 to December 1993. The rest of the 'banking' etc. sector showed no such growth; there, employment grew by only 19 thousand, a rise of less than 1%.

What is even more startling is that the bulk of the alleged employment increase in 'business services n.e.s.' was for full-time males. In 1993 their employment rose by just over 50,000, by 14%, in startling contrast to the considerable fall in full-time male employment in the rest of the economy. A 50,000 rise in full-time male employment by a small and miscellaneous sector is hardly to be passed by without remark; for instance, that number is twice as great as the total of those left in employment in the coal mining industry.

What is the reliable basis for such astounding growth performance?

Indeed, there does not appear to have been one. A 'panel' which covers only 3% of workplaces in the service sector may throw up such bizarre returns. Later issues of the *Employment Gazette* revised 'business services n.e.s.' to lower figures. One would have thought that such unlikely results would have been scrutinised before publication, and the 'panel' overhauled. One is reminded of the exaggerated employment estimates for the finance and other sectors towards the top of the last boom. Why did the Central Statistical Office not fight for improved coverage for the employment estimates (the 'panel') when the last changes were made?

Misrepresenting employment: some conclusions

This chapter has carried a certain amount of technical detail. But what the probing of official figures shows is not a marginal matter.

There is a reluctance to face up to the scale and nature of the falls in employment that have occurred, not least among full-time employees. For Great Britain, full-time employees in employment fell from just over 18 million in mid 1979, to just under 15 million in mid 1994, fifteen years later.

There is a reluctance to offer total figures of employment that show the true 'weight' of part-time employment in terms of 'full-time equivalence'.

There is a reluctance to show openly, alongside the employer-based estimates of employment, just how much double-counting of people at work there is. The recent 'Historical Supplement' of Employment Statistics carries as a footnote under its first table (but not elsewhere) the legend: 'For all dates, individuals with two jobs as employees of different employers are counted twice'. That is perhaps an improvement on total silence. But it does not carry any table conveying such official estimates as do exist. As noticed earlier in this chapter, this double-counting affects nearly 1.2 million individuals today.

As to the self-employed estimates, it must remain an extraordinary 'reform' of these to remove the check against the periodic Census of Employment enumeration of self-employment. And to accompany an arbitrary increase in the published figures of 187,000 with an explanation that denigrates the quality of the full Population Census must rank as unusual official knocking copy. Not least, since what is put in place of the Census is an imperfect sampling process whose doorstep interviewers are clearly briefed to press for almost any element of economically relevant activity to be 'self-assessed' as self-employed.

Nor does it help official credibility to continue to include in the employed work-force total those on 'work related training programmes', when officialdom itself confessed to the 'small contribution' to production involved. This series serves only to remind us that the government is currently supporting, through such programmes, far fewer people preparing through training for future work than when the series was introduced. The 450 thousand in such government programmes in 1989 are reduced to a bare 300 thousand five years later. Like so much else, it signals simply decline.

Nor should we forget the unusual boom in employment — statistically speaking, since the reality cannot be answered for — in 'business services not elsewhere specified' in 1993. This early fruit of the new 'panel' of workplace respondents used in compiling current employment estimates, does not suggest that the worst in unreliability is behind us.

Perhaps official data of this kind on employment should be accompanied by a health, or credibility, warning.

Footnote

1. The June 1994 *Employment Gazette*, page 226, gives approximate confidence intervals: for a size group of 1 million the 95% C.I. is approximately +/- 4.1% (i.e. +/- 4.1%).

CHAPTER FOUR

Young Workers in the Deregulated Economy

John Hughes

I
The 1990s and the collapse
of full-time employment

By the time of the New Earnings Survey in April 1994 there were less than 600,000 young workers aged under 21 still in full-time employment as employees in Great Britain. The previous four years had seen a massive and unprecedented collapse in such full-time employment. In April 1990, at the beginning of the decade, there had been nearly one and a third million young people under 21 who were employees in full-time work. Their number was reduced by almost three-quarters of a million in the four years to 1994, a fall of some 56%. Demography cannot begin to explain this extraordinary fall in full-time work. Official projections (see *Employment Gazette* October 1991) had only implied a fall of some 20% in the numbers of young people 'available' for the labour market. This amounts to the collapse of full-time employment for the young, which affected male and female workers in both manual and non-manual employment. There have been people, not least in government, who have suggested that labour market deregulation and flexibility was a route to higher employment. But in a context of removal of statutory protection and high unemployment, not only did earnings fall in real terms, but there was this immense decline in employment itself.

These estimates derive from the data available from the New Earnings Survey (NES). This survey, which in 1994 analysed returns on a random sample of over 155,000 employees in employment, not only provides immense detail on earnings. Given the nature of its coverage each year, its sample numbers provide a guide as to employment trends. As response rates from employers may vary slightly from year to year, the analysis for this present study has 'grossed up' each set of NES sample numbers to the officially published totals of employees in employment in Britain. There is some element of estimation in this, though it comes from the official employment figures, as well as sub-classifications of the NES data (e.g. by gender, occupation, and age group). But the main directions and scale of change are robustly based.

The main emphasis in what follows is on the comparison between 1990 and 1994, since not only does this cover the most recent period for which information is available, but also because the transformation of employment of young workers is most traumatic then. But to take a longer view, a further analysis of equivalent data for April 1979 has been made. Fortunately the long continuation of the NES on an identical framework makes this possible. (For those who wish to pursue these sources, Part E of the NES offers most of the age-group analysis, and Table 130 is particularly useful for comparative purposes.) So it is possible to take a view of young workers in the labour market which compares their numbers and pay immediately prior to the coming into office of Conservative Governments, with that just over a decade later (in 1990 in a cyclical boom) and with that fifteen years on (in 1994). That decade of the 1980s saw important elements of change in the situation of young workers, but the 1990s have turned out to be a period of very much more sweeping decline in the youth labour market, with not a single redeeming feature in sight.

The New Earnings Survey is a particularly rich source of data on full-time employees. For reasons to do with its basis, which will be explained later, it is a less complete study of part-time employees. Nevertheless it is the richest source of information on part-time female employees (who constitute the great majority of part-time workers). So it is possible not only to explore what happened to full-time employment, but also to extend that study at least to female part-time employment.

The tabulation of findings starts with details of the percentage decline in full-time employment experienced by different age-groups between 1990 and 1994. There is a question as to what age-groups should be included in the notion of 'young workers'. Here it has seemed sensible to include the 21-24 years old age-group as the experience of significant fall in full-time employment applies to this group as well as to the under 21s. It is important also to contrast the experience of younger workers between 1990 and 1994 with that of older workers; so the experience of employment change for all workers (employees in employment) aged 25 and over is included (see Table 1).

A number of important features emerge. One is that the employment fall is most marked for the under 18 age group (where

Table 1
Full-time employees by age-group: estimated percentage changes in employment between April 1990 and April 1994
(Data for Great Britain, for both male and female employees)

Age group	All occupations	Manual occupations	Non-manual occupations
Under 18	-73%	-67%	-78%
18-20	-53%	-51%	-54%
21-24	-17%	-28%	-10%
25 and over	- 5%	-18%	+ 4%

Sources: Estimates derived from sample numbers in NES Part E, Table 130, 1990 and 1994, grossed up to employment estimates for same dates, *Employment Gazette*, Table 1.1.

there is a decline of two-thirds for manual occupations, and one of more than three-quarters for non-manuals). But the decline for the much larger 18-20 age group is also massive and unprecedented, falling by slightly more than a half for both manual and non-manual occupations. It should also be noted that for adult employees aged 25 and over there is a marked contrast. Manual employment continues and extends the persistent decline that was a feature of the 1980s. A fall of 18% for manual full-time employment in only four years is almost certainly a reflection of longer term structural decline as well as cyclical factors (notably the manufacturing recession). By contrast there is a modest expansion of non-manual employment. What is particularly interesting is that there is so much similarity in the exceptional employment decline for the younger age-groups whether they embrace manual or non-manual work, although there is a clear divergence in the trends of adult (manual and non-manual) employment. The 21-24 year olds experience, as shown in Table 1, is intermediate; both occupational categories decline in employment, but non-manual by 10%, compared with nearly 30% for manual employees. Overall, the decline of full-time employment for employees under 25 (all age groups under 25) between 1990 and 1994, was one of 30% for non-manual employees, compared with a 4% growth for age 25 and above; for manual employment the under-25s show an employment decline of 40% overall, compared with an 18% decline for the over-25s. If anything, the differentiation in employment experience for younger as compared with older age-groups, is more extreme in the case of non-manual employment. At this stage it is probably helpful to look at the actual numbers behind these dramatic rates of change. How many jobs are we talking about, and how many young workers in 1994 were still in full-time employment after these years of

Table 2
Estimated changes in numbers of full-time employees, 1990-1994* and numbers in full-time employment in April 1994, by age-group (in thousands) (Data for Great Britain, for both male and female employees)

CHANGE	Under 21	21-24	All under 25	All 25 and over
1990-94				
Manual occupations	-310	-210	-520	-955
Non-manual occupations	-435	-120	-555	+320
All occupations	-745	-330	-1,075	-635
Numbers in full-time employment, April 1994				
Manual occupations	260	540	800	4,430
Non-manual occupations	315	1,100	1,415	8,315
All occupations	575	1,640	2,215	12,745

Sources: As for Table 1.
*April in each year.

shattering job decline? Table 2 offers rounded estimates of the numbers involved, by age-group and by occupational category.

The first column in the top part of Table 2 tells us that there were nearly three-quarters of a million fewer under 21s in full-time employment as employees in 1994, than there had been in 1990. The same column in the bottom half of the Table tells us that there were only some 575,000 under 21s left in full-time employment in 1994. Altogether for all under 25s there was a reduction of more than a million full-time employees over the four years, compared with less than two-thirds of a million for full-time employees aged 25 plus.

Given the rather small sample sizes involved, the Table has grouped together all young workers under 21, but, broadly speaking, the reduction in full-time employment as employees for the age group under 18 was some 180,000 over the four years, and only some 70,000 remained in full-time employment in 1994. For the 18-20 age-group the fall in full-time employment was clearly over half a million, and only just over half a million were in full-time employment at those ages in 1994.

So the disproportionate collapse of employment of younger workers meant that the bulk of the fall in full-time employment in 1990-94, which, for all full-time employees in Britain is officially estimated to have declined by 1.7 million, fell on the shoulders of the under 25s. For the under 25s the decline in both manual and non-manual employment was very similar (a decline of over half a million in each case); for the over 25s a decline of nearly a million manual full-time employees contrasted with an increase of close to one-third of a million in non-manual full-time employment. But in overall terms in 1994 there was one full-time job less for every twenty available in 1990 for adult employees aged 25 and over; for the under 25s in 1994 there was one job less for every three full-time jobs available to young employees in 1990.

Before we reflect on why the deregulated market worked in this way, it is important to look at the labour market experience of young workers in terms of gender. In fact, the experience of young male and female employees seems to have been very similar, insofar as the decline in full-time employment fell even-handedly on both. Proportional rates of fall in full-time employment were more evidently linked to occupation than to gender.

Table 3
Full-time employees by age-group and gender: estimated changes in employment, April 1990 and April 1994 (Great Britain)

Age-group	Males		Females	
	Manual	Non-manual	Manual	Non-manual
Percentage change				
Under 21	-57%	-59%	-50%	-58%
21-24	-29%	- 4%	-25%	-14%
25 and over	-18%	NIL	-16%	+ 9%
Change in numbers (in thousands)				
Under 21	-235	-145	- 75	-290
21-24	-165	- 20	- 45	-100
25 and over	-830	+ 10	-125	+310

Sources: As for Table 1. Estimates rounded.

From a somewhat larger total in employment in 1990, full-time male employment numbers fell by over 560,000 for the under 25s between 1990 and 1994, compared with a fall of just over half a million in full-time female employees' numbers for those age groups.

By 1994 there were just over 1.1 million males in full-time employment aged under 25, compared with just under 1.1 million females. Above the age range of younger workers, for those aged 25 plus, the years from 1990 to 1994 saw a major fall in adult male employment (which was entirely concentrated on manual workers) and a modest rise in female employment, concentrated on non-manual employment.

At this stage it is important to ask, was the traumatic decline in full-time employment that affected every category of young worker between 1990 and 1994 the continuation of earlier trends — albeit at a more hectic pace? Or were there categories of younger workers, or particular age-groups, for whom this was an experience of employment decline sharply different to earlier years?

The age-group for which it might be argued that the contraction of full-time employment was no novelty is the under 18 year olds. In round terms, their numbers in full-time employment had fallen by 60% between 1979 and 1990, to no more than a quarter of a million. Population change and patterns of school leaving pointed to a fall of around a quarter in age-group numbers over the decade. So the availability of full-time jobs seems to have turned emphatically against the youngest workers in that earlier period. Even so, that earlier process of employment decline represents the outcome of a whole decade; the four years, 1990 to 1994, accelerated to a rate of decline of over 70%. The 'big battalions' of young people in full-time employment back in 1979 were males under 18 in manual work, and females under 18 in non-manual employment; their combined numbers can be estimated to have fallen from near half a million in 1979 to around 50,000 by 1994. That is a shattering phenomenon in social terms, not least in areas previously dominated by male manual work.

The massive decline of full-time employees age 18-20 in employment that developed between 1990-1994 (a decline of 50% and more for all categories in that age-group, males and females, manual and non-manual occupations) has much less by way of precedent. Between 1979 and 1990, full-time employment for this age-group had fallen by around one-quarter. Only males in manual employment had a steeper fall in employment than that — a fall of 35% over the eleven years to 1990 (less surprising, given the fall of around one-quarter in overall male manual employment over that period). But this contrasted with a fall in full-time employment of only around 10% for non-manual males in that age-group between 1979 and 1990. So there was nothing in earlier experience that foreshadowed the cutting in half of full-time employment for employees in this 18-20 age-group (a decline of well over half a million full-time jobs) between 1990 and 1994.

The same sense of an adverse and unexpected shift in the behaviour of the labour market is apparent in the 1990s for the 21-24 age-group. In the previous decade (comparing 1979 with 1990) there appears to have been an increase in their full-time employment. The numbers of 21-24 year old employees in full-time employment rose overall by some 6% to stand just under two million. Only young men in manual work showed a modest decline (of 10%) over that period. Both male and female non-manual full-time employment of 21-24 year olds had increased over the 1980s (women non-manual employees by some 15%) and so had employment of manual women. So that, when from 1990 to 1994 there were declines in full-time employment for all these categories of 21-24 year old employees, and major falls in particular for men and women manual workers and for women non-manual workers, we are confronting a serious and substantially new social and economic phenonemon. The fall in full-time employment of some 330,000 between 1990 and 1994 for that age-group extends our perception of employment for young workers into that age range. Although the fall in manual employment was the more severe, the 10% fall in non-manual full-time employment for the 21-24s contrasted not only with earlier experience, but also with increased employment for older non-manual employees (25 and over) in the very same years of the 1990s.

At this stage, it may be important to stand back from the employment data to ask whether deregulated (and cyclically depressed) markets were demonstrating a massive collapse in demand for young workers, or whether employers were confronting supply-side problems — whether from reduction of supply or excessively high pay requirements. The earnings issues are explored in the next section of this chapter. At this stage, all that need be said is that young workers pay was low in comparative terms, and earnings in the 1990s were falling in 'real' terms. But even this did not prevent the steep decline in employment. As to numbers on the supply side, there was a fall in the total population in these age-groups during this period of the early 1990s. It was greater for the 18-20 age group (approaching 20%) than for 20-24 year olds (under 10%). And in face of highly adverse labour market conditions numbers of young people in further and higher education grew. But the telling refutation of any idea that employers faced a supply-side 'shortage' of young workers comes from official unemployment data. Even granted that claimant unemployed statistics understate the true extent of unemployment, an increase in recorded unemployment must strengthen the argument for the jobs decline being rooted in a collapse in employers' demand for young people in full-time employment.

The *Employment Gazette* carries a detailed age and duration analysis for claimant unemployment for April 12th, 1990, and for April 14th, 1994 (See *Employment Gazette*, Table 2.6). The age-groups chosen do not coincide exactly with those of the New Earnings Survey, but aggregate figures can be provided for the age range 18 to 24, both for employment estimates from the New Earnings Survey, and unemployment figures on the 'claimants' basis from the *Employment Gazette*; in both cases it is returns for Great Britain that are being compared. The NES based estimate for April

1990 is for just over 3 million young workers in full-time employment as employees in the age range 18-24. At the same time there were 439,000 'claimant unemployed' in the same age range. Since claimants are required to be seeking and available for full-time employment, it is useful to compare the two totals. By spring 1994 the equivalent number of full-time employees in employment in the same age-range had fallen by 900,000 to a little over 2.1 million. At the same time, the unemployed numbers aged 18-24 had risen to 700,000 (a rise of 60%). The evidence, then, is overwhelming; the labour market for young workers was characterised by high recorded unemployment in 1990, and their numbers had swollen much further (by more than an additional quarter of a million) by 1994. The traumatic falls in employment over those years were accompanied by very high and steeply rising unemployment.

It would seem impossible to record this and pass on without emphasizing the sheer neglect and waste of our younger generation that such figures — understated as they are — actually involve. For instance, the numbers dwarf the old vocabulary that spoke of the 'reserve army' of the unemployed. 'Reserve army'!: in 1994 the numbers of service personnel in H.M's whole army, navy, and airforce only totalled 36% of those young people aged 18-24 that stood unemployed. Within that vast total of the excluded, those who talk of an opportunity state should notice especially the 'experience' of long term unemployment that is being recorded. Taking only the young men aged 20-24 who had been 'claimant' unemployed for a year or more; in April 1990 there were 50,000 of them who represented a combined experience of around 111,000 years of unemployment. By April 1994 there were 124,500 young men aged 20-24 who had then recorded more than a year's continuous unemployment by the survey date; between them this represented around 274,000 years of the experience of continuous unemployment. This 'long term' unemployment in 1994 was two and a half times as great as in 1990.

Yet the unemployment of young workers in 1990 had already been disproportionately high (the young workers in 1990 aged 18-24 were some 18% of all full-time employees in employment, but the unemployment in that age-group was 29% of the British total).

The situation of young male employees has, in particular, to be recognised. In 1990, with over 1.5 million male employees in employment on a full-time basis (aged between 18 and 24), there was already an attendant mass unemployment of 300,000. By April 1994, full-time employment for these young men had fallen by 450 thousand to under 1.1 million; the attendant unemployment had risen by 200,000 to close to half a million. This group accounted for only 7% of total full-time employment in Britain in 1994, but 19% of claimant unemployment. This is how Mr Major's economy manages one of its most important resources.

Of course, many young people trapped in this savagely negative labour market have poured, in increasing numbers, into school sixth forms, FE Colleges, and Universities, all of which have been provided with diminished and diminishing per capita real resources. Their ability to cope effectively with the development needs of many of their students must be in doubt; one suspects that many of those young people who are most vulnerable in labour market terms will also be least able to avoid 'failure' in an educational system under intense pressure. It is all too evident that the real failure lies elsewhere.

Before leaving the analysis of employment it is important to piece together evidence of the scale (and motivation) of part-time work by young workers. The nature of the NES sample, which is based on Inland Revenue pay-as-you-earn (PAYE) returns, means that its coverage of part-time workers is incomplete, and as the exclusion relates to workers below the income tax threshold (in 1994, earnings of 53.50 a week) this affects a proportion of young workers, due, not only to low hourly pay, but to a small number of hours worked. The NES does, however, provide some detailed coverage of female part-time workers. Other survey data is available through the Labour Force Survey.

What the part-time data do show is that although part-time work has grown, its expansion (mostly in the 21-24 age group) is modest in scale, and is far from replacing full-time employment. So far as part-time male employment is concerned, a spring 1994 LFS survey estimated 365 thousand in part-time employment aged 16-24. Nearly 80% of these were students (that is, around 290 thousand). Less than 60 thousand said they were in part-time work because they couldn't find a full-time job. Most of those who were in part-time work while being students, worked very short hours — over half of them ten hours a week, or fewer. All in all, the part-time work by young workers aged 24 and under would probably have amounted to only a little over 100 thousand full-time equivalents, so far as males were concerned. (Data in this paragraph is from an article in *Employment Gazette*, December 1994, on 'Part-time Working').

The same LFS survey estimated (spring 1994) 575 thousand female employees working part-time, aged between 16 and 24. Some 328 thousand of these were students; 109 thousand said they were working part-time because they couldn't find a full-time job. For female employees, as for male, those who were students working part-time, in the main worked very short working weeks. 70% of such students worked 10 hours or fewer. Overall, the part-time work when expressed as full-time equivalents (FTEs) would have amounted to some 200 thousand.

The New Earnings Survey provides some indication as to patterns of change in part-time work between 1990 and 1994, for female employees. For manual part-time work there is no evidence of increased numbers in the 18-20 age-group, but by 1994 a higher proportion than in 1990 were working very short weekly hours. For those aged 21-24 there is an increase in numbers of around 30 thousand between 1990 and 1994, but with some shift towards fewer weekly hours worked. For non-manual females there is data for part-timers under 18; this shows stable numbers (around 50 thousand) and very limited hours, with nearly 60% working only 8 hours or less a week. The 18-20 age-group sample numbers indicate a rise of some 25 thousand to close to 80 thousand in part-time employment in 1994. In both 1990 and 1994, weekly hours for the majority of such employees are short, with two-thirds working 16 hours or less. The 21-24 age-group is characterised by large numbers in part-time work (over 150 thousand) and a sharp increase in such work (approaching 70 thousand) by 1994. But here, too, there was a shift to fewer weekly hours worked, and in 1994 nearly half worked 16 hours or less.

On this evidence, the main expansion in part-time employment of young workers in the 1990s appears to have occurred in the 21-24 age-group, where an increase of female employment in all occupations of around 100,000 can be estimated from the (incomplete) NES data. In full-time equivalents this might represent an increase of around 40,000. It is clear that this is not a major offset to the immense decline in full-time employment of young workers.

II
Earnings and incomes of young workers in the 1990s

This chapter has shown what deregulated labour markets have done to the employment, and especially the full-time employment, of young workers in the 1990s. But what has deregulation brought young workers in terms of earnings? There is a need, in exploring this subject, to find a way in which underlying trends in earnings for different groups of workers at different times can be simply and reasonably conveyed.

What is done here is to come as close as possible to identifying 'basic' earnings per week. The New Earnings Survey actually has a table (Table 130) which enables this to be done, with direct comparisons between different periods of time. It separates out from total weekly earnings the elements of overtime pay, payments by results elements, and shift premia. The residual category it terms 'all other weekly pay'. This enables us to be less concerned with seeking to make comparisons at the same point in a business cycle.

Secondly, it is possible to make allowances for changes in the purchasing power of pay due to inflation. This is referred to as making comparisons at 'constant prices'; the most suitable index for this purpose is the Retail Prices Index (RPI). This has been used to compare the purchasing power of gross pay as between April 1990 and April 1994. (The RPI rose by 17.4% between March 1990 and March 1994.) It has to be recognised that this still does not indicate how far tax changes, etc., may have altered disposable income over a period of time. But it does offer a realistic comparison of weekly pay at different points in time.

To begin with, it is useful to establish how the basic earnings of young workers have changed over the period — and the period since 1979 has been one of deregulation and widening inequalities in pay — in comparison with those of adult workers generally. Table 4 does this by contrasting, for 'all other weekly pay', the NES recorded weekly earnings of workers aged 18-20 in full-time employment, and that of adult workers aged 21 and over in full-time employment. Both sets of figures are arithmetic averages.

The message of the Table is clear. For all categories there has been a considerable relative decline in the earnings of 18-20 year olds; male or female, manual or non-manual, the relative decline of their average earnings in relation to those of adult full-time

Table 4
Comparative earnings of full-time employees aged 18-20 and those aged 21 and over: 1979, 1990, and 1994 ('All other weekly pay')

Average pay of 18-20 year olds as percentage of that of 21 plus

Years	Manual male	Manual female
1979	78%	87%
1990	72%	83%
1994	68%	82%

Years	Non-manual male	Non-manual female
1979	49%	70%
1990	42%	62%
1994	39%	54%

Source: Data from NES Table 130 for the relevant years.

employees is strongly marked and is taken further in the 1990s. If the decline appears more modest in the case of the smallest category, female manual employees, this is because the overall level of earnings is particularly low, and there is little by way of skill or career progression. Since there are now so few under 18s in full-time employment, the findings in their case have not been separately tabulated. But for the largest segment of under 18s, male manuals, the comparative level of earnings (in relation to average earnings of adult male manual workers) fell from 55% in 1979 to 49% in 1990, and then to 44% in 1994. We are looking at the same pattern of relative decline.

After this, it is not so surprising to find that between 1990 and 1994 the average ('all other pay') weekly earnings of full-time employees actually fell in 'constant price' terms, with the one exception of female manual employees, over a period in which their adult counterparts showed some positive real earnings growth. Table 5 provides the detail.

Table 5
Average earnings of full-time employees by age-group, gender, and occupation in April 1994, and percentage change in constant price average weekly earnings, 1990-1994

(All other weekly pay)

Age group	Male		Female	
	Manual	Non-manual	Manual	Non-Manual
April 1994: average earnings in £				
Under 18	£ 96.8	£112.2	£101.8	£114.7
18-20	£147.6	£155.7	£128.0	£145.1
21 and over	£217.7	£399.5	£156.8	£269.7
Percentage change in average earnings, 1990-94, at constant prices				
Under 18	-5.5%	-7.4%	+2.0%	-6.5%
18-20	-1.8%	-4.8%	+3.2%	-5.2%
21 and over	+3.9%	+2.2%	+5.2%	+8.5%

Sources: NES Table 130. *Employment Gazette*. See text for explanation of 'all other weekly pay'.

So far as the modest increases in adult weekly earnings are concerned, the only unusual feature is the limited advance in the 'constant price' earnings of non-manual men; perhaps the thinning out of expensive hierarchies in, for example, the finance sector has played its part. But the faster advance in non-manual women's pay has been a constant feature of the last fifteen years.

Not so, however, the pay of the youngest age groups of

non-manual female workers. Of course, with the enormous fall in full-time employment for the youngest groups, we may be looking at a different occupational pattern within their sector for those that are left. But in terms that de-regulated markets can understand, it could hardly be said that 'inflexibility' of pay has been a barrier to employment. Young people's earnings have lost out both relatively (to their older equivalents) and absolutely (in relation to the faster advance of price inflation than of their nominal pay). There seem to have been no compensating benefits of any kind for young workers in the Thatcherite — and then the Majorite — version of labour markets. Except perhaps the demonstration that this was clearly not the route to job creation. This still leaves out the administrative distortions that young workers, and would-be workers, have been subjected to; the training for non-existent jobs as officialdom presides over a continuing holocaust of jobs (not least the choking off of socially beneficial public sector employment); the pressure on the unemployed for job search as jobs disappeared in the 1990s by the hundred thousand.

There is one further dimension of importance. The massive loss of jobs and the weakness in earnings levels, taken together, have drastically reduced the aggregate income of young people from full-time work. We can make some estimates of the scale of this; it has macro-economic implications. For instance, the aggregate earnings from full-time employment of young employees under 21 were, in 1994, not much more than 40% of their (constant price) level in 1990. In annual terms this looks like a decline in 1994 prices, of over £5,000 million a year to an amount of around £4,200 million. We can add to these figures some allowance for the fall in aggregate income from full-time employment as a result of the reduction in jobs for 21-24 year old employees. (Their average earnings between 1990 and 1994 only rose around 1% in constant prices, so this was a negligible offset to the employment decline.) The reduction in their total incomes from full-time employment between 1990 and 1994 would be, in 1994 prices, well over £3,000 million. Taking all the young workers in full-time employment under 25, the job loss and earnings experience between 1990 and 1994 must have reduced annual gross earnings by not far short of £9,000 million a year by 1994.

Of course, this loss of income did not stand on its own. It is being reinforced by curtailments of benefit income, student grants, etc. Perhaps the government would like to calculate the net result. But it must make it difficult to talk as if some revival of a 'feel good' factor only needs a little more cyclical expansion (though that is being choked off by higher interest rates too).

Is it so surprising that the 'first time buyer' housing market is so flat, when young workers' incomes have been so massively deflated (though, of course, the housing market is being further choked off by the same rising interest rates)? Is it surprising that homelessness is everywhere more evident? And is it so surprising that under these conditions it is not easy to form stable households, or indeed to shield the next generation of children from poverty? Perhaps at some point there will be an attempt to recognise the high social and economic costs of subjecting the rising generation to a deregulated labour market dominated by short-termism, and, as in the early 1990s, lurching through a dangerously unstable business cycle made worse by incompetent government management of the economy. But in any case, our rising generation should not forgive nor forget the injustice and denial of opportunity that this has represented.

CHAPTER FIVE

Crime and Unemployment

John Wells[1]

Introduction

Britain's departure from full employment in the mid-1970s and the subsequent emergence of mass unemployment on a scale not witnessed since the 1930s, together with increasing inequality in the distribution of income amongst the employed and between the employed and the unemployed have coincided with a strong trend rise in recorded crime — the cause of much public anxiety. Indeed, public opinion surveys show crime and unemployment vying with each other for top place amongst the voters' principal concerns.

Common sense suggests how unemployment and crime might be causally related. Unemployment provides the *motivation* — in the form of absolute and relative material deprivation (in a society setting great store by material success), frustrated aspirations, boredom and anger; whilst the generally high level of material possessions enjoyed by the vast majority who remain in work provides the *opportunity*. All that is missing from a purely economic account of the causes of property crime is the loosening of the individual's moral or ethical constraints on unlawful behaviour (personal conscience). But, the growing sense of illegitimacy of an economic and social order that countenances mass unemployment and increasing inequality might provide just the solvent to loosen those constraints.

Of course, not all unemployed individuals resort to crime; indeed, a great deal of crime is committed by youngsters still in school as by those in work — indeed, whilst they are actually at work. And retired people also contribute in some small measure to the crime statistics! And, whilst few would suggest that economic hardship is the sole determinant of crime, there appears, nonetheless, to be an important role for economic factors. Thus, an attempt to identify the precursors of delinquent behaviour, using data from a longitudinal survey of roughly 400 white inner city males born in 1953 (Farrington *et al* (1988)) — admittedly largely undertaken during an era of relatively full employment — found a role for economic deprivation (low family income, unemployment/job instability and poor housing) together with poor parenting, family criminality and school failure. And this accords with popular common sense and experience.

It is even more likely that the current era of mass unemployment, with high spatial concentrations and long average durations, is fostering conditions of economic and social deprivation and blighted aspirations which are a fertile breeding-ground for crime — not just amongst the unemployed themselves but amongst the children and juveniles of the affected neighbourhoods.

Successive Conservative governments since 1979 have strongly resisted the idea of a causal link running from unemployment to crime, even during the inner city riots and disorder which accompanied spiralling unemployment during the recessions of the early 1980s and 1990s. The reasons for this are easy to discern. First, having presided over the slide into mass unemployment, admitting such a link also implies culpability for the crime wave as well. Second, government has eschewed all responsibility for the level of unemployment, arguing that its role is limited to creating an appropriate environment for encouraging job creation; but, if unemployment is causally linked to crime, this denial of responsibility is greatly at variance with the government's commitment to the maintenance of 'law and order'. Finally, governments since 1979 have resorted to increasing unemployment as a policy instrument designed to counter inflation — as evidenced by Chancellor Lamont's remark that 'unemployment is a price well worth paying'. If unemployment is causally linked to crime, then the costs of the latter would need to be factored into any cost-benefit analysis of whether resort to such a barbarous instrument of economic policy can be justified in terms of any putative economic pay-off.

Members of the government have sought support for their views in influential research undertaken at the Home Office by Simon Field (1990a). However, as we argue in this chapter, the statistical evidence linking crime and unemployment is much stronger than is commonly supposed, and Home Office research can be criticized on numerous grounds.

Crime statistics:
the main facts and statistical pitfalls

The crime statistics which hit the newspaper headlines are typically those of indictable offences reported by the general public to the police and recorded by them — published regularly in *Criminal*

Statistics: England & Wales.[2] However, not all crime is reported by the public — nor do the police record every crime that is: thus, there is a leakage in the statistics at each stage as one moves from the 'true' or underlying level of crime to those crimes reported by the public and then to crime as recorded by the police. So-called 'victimization' surveys (that for England & Wales being the household-based *British Crime Survey*[3]) provide a more accurate estimate than police records of the 'true' level of crime for most types of offences.[4] Comparing police records with the *BCS* provides a good idea of the extent of the 'dark figure' of crime i.e. that which goes unreported or, if reported, unrecorded. Highest in terms of degree of coverage provided by police records are theft of vehicles (93%) and household burglary with loss (68%)[5] — basically reflecting insurance companies' requirements on reporting. Intermediate in terms of the coverage of police records are: theft from a motor vehicle (32%), wounding (25%) and robbery (23%). Whilst vandalism, with only 1 in 7 cases finding their way into police records, and 'theft from the person' (1 in 11 cases) have the lowest degrees of police recording.

However, both sources concur that, considering serious ('indictable') offences, crimes against property (burglary, theft, fraud and forgery, criminal damage [vandalism] and robbery) dwarf by a factor of 22:1 crimes against the person (violence against the person,[6] including homicide, and sexual offences) — albeit crimes against the person are of understandably of great concern to the general public. Crimes against property involve, on average, losses which, though not trivial, could , in no way, be described as enormous[7] (£984 averaged over all burglaries both residential and non-residential;[8] £973 averaged over all thefts including motor vehicle theft and shoplifting) — though even small sums can occasion considerable stress to the vicims involved.

An obvious question which arises in respect of police recorded crimes, which are those normally informing newspaper headlines, is whether possible increases in the extent of reporting (due to: insurance requirements, the spread of telephone ownership and apparently greater sensitivity to crime and lower tolerance towards anti-social behaviour amongst the general public) as well as changes in police recording practice have exaggerated the extent of the crime 'wave' in recent decades — thereby alarming the public unduly? Data on the underlying or 'true' level of crime obtained from the *BCS* can be used to answer this question. Crime overall has definitely been on a rising trend[9] (increasing by 49% or 4.1% p.a. between 1981-91 according to the *BCS*) — though but not by as much as suggested by police records (a rise of 96% or 7.0% p.a.

between 1981-91). On the rise in acquisitive or property offences, police records and the *BCS* broadly agree on an increase of about 95% or 6.9% p.a. between 1981-91 (increased reporting by the public being offset by a decline in police recording); 'true' levels of violence against the person increased by 21% and vandalism was flat (according to the *BCS*) — compared with a doubling under both counts according to police records. Thus, public perceptions that the 1980s saw an upsurge in crime is supported by the *BCS*; but it was largely concentrated in property crime, whilst the increase in violence against the person was modest and that in vandalism non-existent.[10]

Victims of residential burglary, as recorded by the 1992 *BCS*, are likely to live in council estates or mixed inner city residential areas (i.e. where the rich live cheek by jowl with the poor) or high-status non-family areas or older terraced houses; risk factors associated with car theft, on the other hand, seem to be: inner city residence, higher household income, 'consumerist' tendencies.

Offenders are overwhelmingly male and young. Data on known offenders (i.e. those found guilty by the courts or cautioned by police) show: (i) males between the ages of 17 and 25 accounted for 69.7% of total adult convictions and cautions and 48.5% of all convictions and cautions for burglary committed in 1990; (ii) offending rates for men rising rapidly from age 10 to a peak between the age of 17 and 18 (in 1992)[11] after which they decline — as less time is spent in the company of other men and under the influence of marriage.[12] Information on self-reported offending indicates a somewhat lower peak age.[13] The scale of offending by young men is best summarized by the following statistic: by the time they have reached their thirty-first birthday, roughly one third of all young men have received at least one criminal conviction. This conclusion is derived from longitudinal surveys of cohorts of randomly-chosen males born in 1953, 1958 and 1963 (Shaw and Lobo (1989)). Moreover, conviction rates appear to be increasing for successive cohorts — despite falling conviction rates for juvenile (age 10-16 years) offenders due to the increased use of cautions and warnings. Additionally, a relatively small proportion of offenders, dubbed 'chronic' offenders, are responsible for a totally disproportionate share of crime; thus, 5% of men in the cohorts referred to above accounted for two-thirds of all convictions. Such 'chronic' offenders tend to start early their life of crime. Thus, the younger the male offender at his first conviction, the higher the probability of re-conviction and the longer his criminal career: of those males first convicted between the ages of 8 and 14, a quarter were convicted on more than five occasions during the subsequent ten year period;

whereas of those first convicted at age 20, almost two-thirds avoided a further conviction during the next ten years.[14]

Conviction rates for men are much higher than for women. Men are more likely to be convicted of theft (other than shoplifting), burglary and criminal damage; women are more likely to be convicted of shoplifting.

The final statistic worth noting concerns the employment status of known offenders. Tarling (1982) reported that 'research studies of known offenders had repeatedly shown that somewhere in the region of four out of ten were unemployed: a much higher proportion than in the population as a whole'. Data collected by the Northumbria police (Northumbria Police (1977), (1978), (1980)) show the proportion of detected crime involving unemployed people rose for total crime from 26% (1975) to 49% (1980) and for burglary from 31% (1975) to 56% (1980) at a time when claimant unemployment rose from 5.3% in 1975 to 12.1% in 1980. From these figures it is clear: (i) the unemployed are responsible for a disproportionate share of crime relative to their numbers in the population; (ii) the probability of an unemployed individual being detected as having committed a crime is at least 10 times that of an employed person; (iii) unemployed men aged 16 to 29 years committed 39.4% of all detected crime in 1980 and 49.1% of all burglaries.

Testing for the crime-unemployment relationship: methodological issues

Empirical studies of the crime-unemployment relationship are typically of one or other of two types: first, *aggregate* or *macro* studies that examine the relationship for groups of individuals (e.g nations, regions etc.), using either *time series* data (i.e. data through time for a given country, region) or *cross section* data (data for different regions, cities etc. at a given point in time) or combining both.[15] The alternative *micro* approach draws on information about individuals, typically of a longitudinal kind (i.e. over the course of time), and examines the correlates of offending behaviour (e.g. the incidence of offending behaviour during spells of unemployment compared with spells of employment). *Aggregate* studies are more numerous since statistical data in that form is extremely abundant reflecting the fact that most of the data gathered by official statistical agencies is in this form. *Micro* studies are relatively few in number since they are based on longitudinal studies which are expensive to undertake and few and far between. Each approach has its own advantages and disadvantages.[16]

The empirical evidence presented in this paper is based on *aggregate* data. We present and analyze *time series* data for Britain (for England & Wales and Scotland) on criminal offences and various indicators of economic activity for the period since 1970 — which is when the British economy first began to depart from full employment. We also present *cross-section* data for 41 police force areas in England & Wales on certain property crimes and claimant unemployment in 1992. Finally, combining *time-series* and *cross-section* data, we examine the relationship between changes in household burglary and changes in unemployment between 1975 and 1992 for 41 police force areas in England and Wales.

This note does not attempt to summarize all the previous research on the crime-unemployment relationship, whether for the UK or elsewhere.[17] However, it does seek to build on and extend recent contributions to the study of this relationship in the UK context — notably by Field (1990a), Timbrell (1988), Dickinson (1994) and Carr-Hill and Stern (1979).

Property crime and the economic cycle

That property crime is sensitive to fluctuations in economic activity — growing rapidly when the economy is in the doldrums and growing less rapidly or even declining when the economy is performing well — is a well-established proposition empirically supported by evidence from numerous countries over varying time periods. Indeed, one can say that, amongst those who have examined UK data on the matter in recent times, there is near universal agreement that property crime moves inversely with the economic cycle. Simon Field (1990), the Home Office researcher, after drawing attention to an older historical tradition of thought on the subject, represented by Von Mayr (quoted in Mannheim (1965)), Bonger (1916), Thomas (1925) and Radzinowicz (1971), has done as much as any researcher in modern times to establish, in the case of Britain's own historical experience, the sensitivity of property crime, measured from police records, to the economic cycle. Thus, he finds evidence of a statistical association between year-on-year changes in property crime and economic circumstances from 1860 up to the present day.[18]

The evidence for the two decades or so since 1970 is particularly persuasive. Figure 1 plots annual data on total indictable (or serious) property offences,[19] from police records, for England & Wales for the period 1950-93, whilst Figure 2 plots annual data for Scotland[20] on total crimes of dishonesty[21] for 1971-92. Two conclusions stand out clearly. First, property crime, measured from police records,

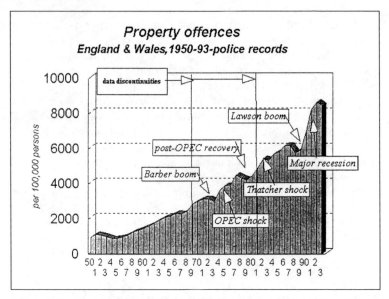

Figure 1: England & Wales, 1950-93: all property crime (offences per 100,000 population)

exhibits a strong upward trend as Britain leaves full employment behind and makes the transition to an era of mass unemployment. Second, recorded property offences, albeit rising strongly during the period 1970-93 as a whole, actually fell during each of the up-turns in economic activity since 1970: during the Barber boom of 1972-3, during the partial economic recovery of 1978-79 towards the end of the last Labour administration and during the most intense phase of the Lawson boom (1988-89) and, finally, during 1993 as output recovery got underway.[22] Conversely, recorded property crime rose strongly and exhibited above-trend increases during each of the down-turns in economic activity: during the recession of the mid-1970s following the first OPEC price shock, during the Thatcher-Howe recession of the early 1980s caused by the twin economic shocks of monetary and fiscal deflation and real sterling exchange rate appreciation and also during the Major economic recession of the early 1990s.

This relationship between total recorded property crime and the economic cycle — whereby property crime actually falls during the recovery phase of the economic cycle and rises during recessions — is confirmed by the time series graphs for England & Wales for virtually all the separate components included within 'property crime': total burglary (Figure 3), both household burglary (Figure

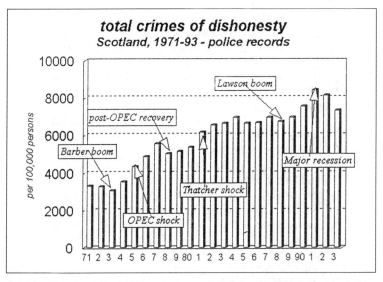

Figure 2: Scotland, 1971-93: total crimes of dishonesty — police records (per 100,000 population)

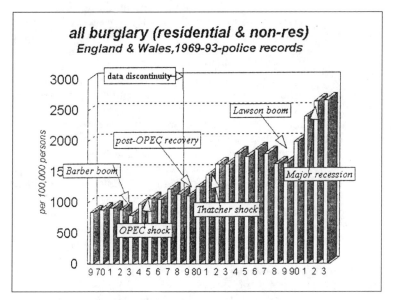

Figure 3: England & Wales: total burglaries (residential and non-residential) (per 100,000 population)

4) and non-residential (Figure 5); total theft and handling of stolen goods (Figure 6), theft of a motor vehicle (Figure 7), theft from a motor vehicle (Figure 8); shoplifting (Figure 9), theft of a pedal cycle (Figure 10) and other theft/unauthorized taking (Figure 11); robbery (Figure 12) and fraud and forgery (Figure 13).

Time series data for Scotland for two of the components of total crimes of dishonesty, housebreaking (Figure 14) and theft of a motor vehicle (Figure 15), shows the same sensitivity to the business cycle.

The evidence in support of the sensitivity of property crime to the economic cycle since 1970 is so pervasive and applies in the case of so many separate crime categories in both England & Wales and Scotland considered separately that it must be hailed as one of the great regularities of modern social and economic statistics.

Development during the 1950s and 1960s (see Figure 1) also require a brief discussion — if only because they appear to be at such variance with the post-1970 experience. Recorded property crime, after registering a strong fall during the first half of the 1950s (a period of exceptionally full employment), increased regularly year-on-year until the early 1970s — with only one year (1967) in which the rising trend was broken. Economic life, on the other hand, was characterized by the so-called 'stop-go' cycle — though such cycles were far less intense in terms of both amplitude and duration than cycles since 1970. Unemployment, though on average very low, exhibited considerable fluctuations. However, there is no evidence using police records for the period 1950-69 of any statistical association between year-to-year variations in property crime (around a strongly-rising trend) and fluctuations in economic activity — however the latter is represented (whether by changes in macro-economic aggregates, such as GDP per head or consumption per head, or changes in labour market variables, such as unemployment).[23] That recorded property crime rose so strongly between the mid-1950s and the early 1970s, a period of rapidly-increasing prosperity, and at year-to-year rates which bear no relationship to fluctuations in economic activity (albeit such fluctuations were relatively modest in the light of subsequent experience) has caused some commentators to question whether adverse economic conditions are a breeding-ground for crime;[24] at the very least, even if recorded property crime is sensitive to the economic cycle from the early 1970s onwards, the experience of the 1950s and 1960s requires some explanation. However, the failure to identify any association between property crime and the business cycle during this earlier period may be ascribed to what is universally agreed to be an important data issue: increased reporting (to the police) and increased recording (by the police) of

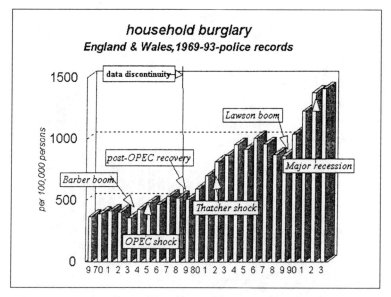

Figure 4: England & Wales, 1969-93: residential burglary (per 100,000 population)

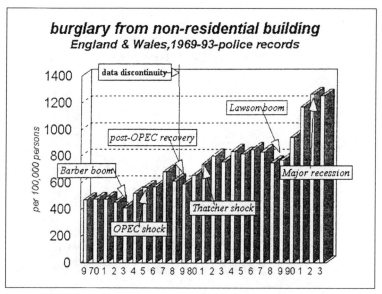

Figure 5: England & Wales, 1969-93: burglary from non-residential building (per 100,000 population)

Figure 6: England & Wales, 1969-93: all theft and handling of stolen goods (per 100,000 population)

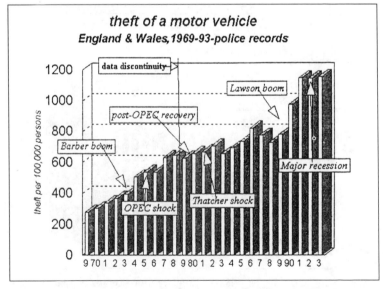

Figure 7: England & Wales, theft of a motor vehicle (per 100,000 population)

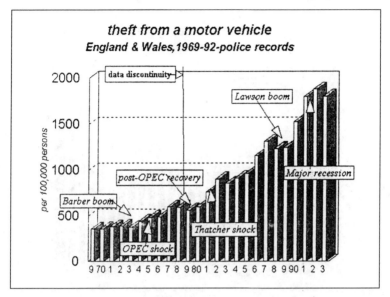

Figure 8: England & Wales, 1969-93; theft from a motor vehicle (per 100,000 population)

Figure 9: England & Wales, 1969-93: shoplifting (per 100,000 population)

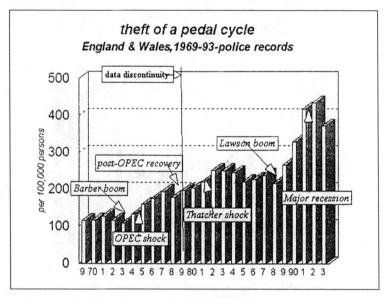

Figure 10: England & Wales, 1969-93: theft of a pedal cycle (per 100,000 population)

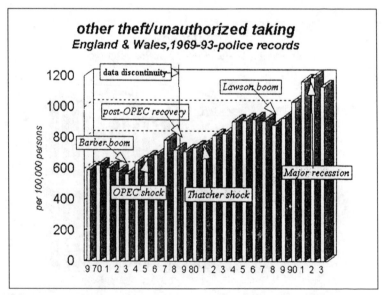

Figure 11: England & Wales, 1969-93: other theft/unauthorised taking (per 100,000 population)

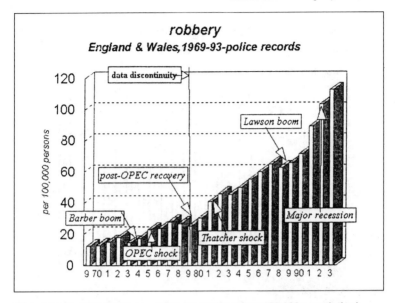

Figure 12: England & Wales, 1969-93: robbery (per 100,000 population)

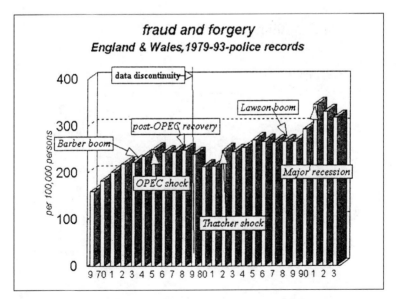

Figure 13: England & Wales, 1969-93: fraud and forgery (per 100,000 population)

Figure 14: Scotland, 1972-93: housebreaking — police records (per 100,000 population)

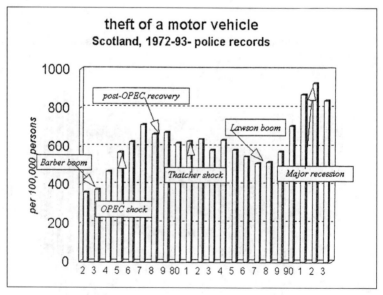

Figure 15: Scotland, 1972-93: theft of motor vehicle — police records (per 100,000 population)

crime due to a number of factors, including: increased police recruitment, greater formalization of procedures, changing public attitudes towards the reporting of crime and the spread of household insurance and telephone ownership. The strong trend increase in the reporting/recording ratio during this period not only means that offences, as measured by police records, overstate the true underlying increase in crime (even to the extent of calling into question whether there really was a crime 'wave' during these decades),[25] but increases in reporting/recording could have been such as to obscure year-to-year fluctuations in underlying offences as well.

Three data issues:
(i) changes in reporting/recording crime

Would property crime's sensitivity to the business cycle since 1970, as measured from police records, which are possibly subject to reporting/recording bias over time, still hold were victimization data, such as that available from the *British Crime Survey* available — the latter providing a more reliable estimate of the 'true' level of crime for many offences. As noted earlier, data from the *1992 BCS* (Mayhew *et al* (1993)) indicate that, in the case of acquisitive or property crimes, which are the main focus of this study, police records appear to provide an unbiased estimate of the growth of crime — at least since 1981 (p.21).[26] Moreover, the coverage provided by police records (relative to the *BCS*) in the case of motor vehicle theft (93%) and burglaries with loss (68%) (p.115-116) — two property crimes of the greatest importance numerically — are very high because of insurance companies' requirements. Thus, we can have a fair measure of confidence in the police time series on property crime.

In addition, it is possible to combine data from the *BCS* with information extracted from the *General Household Survey* question on household burglary, asked since the early 1970s, to obtain the best estimate available of the trend and fluctuations in household burglary for England & Wales (see Figure 16).[27] It confirms the sensitivity of household burglary to the business cycle established from police records. Household burglary declines during the Barber boom (1973), increases during the Thatcher-Howe recession of the early 1980s, falls rapidly during the Lawson boom and shoots up again during the Major recession of the early 1990s. This is probably the most persuasive piece of evidence available of the sensitivity of property crime to the business cycle.

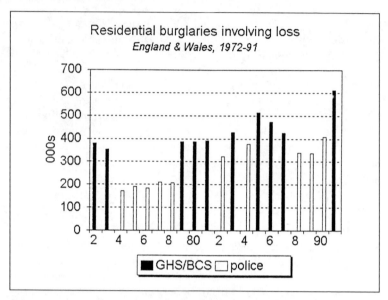

**Figure 16: England & Wales, 1972-91: residential burglaries involving loss
— data from *General Household Survey/British Crime Survey* and police
records**

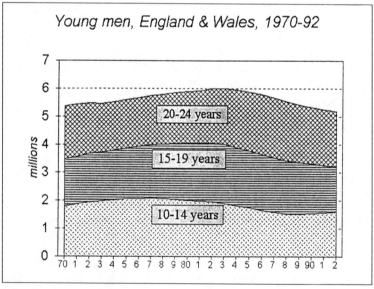

**Figure 17: England & Wales, 1970-92: numbers of young men in the population
(millions)**

Data issues: (ii) demographic developments — a declining number of young men in the population in the late 1980s

One obvious explanation for the decline in property crime during the Lawson boom of the latter half of the 1980s suggests itself. As noted earlier, the peak age of offending for young men (using data on those cautioned or found guilty in courts) is between 17 and 18;[28] and whilst information on those cautioned or found guilty may be unrepresentative of offenders taken as a whole, data on self-reported offences locate the peak offending rate at an even younger age.[29] During the 1980s demographic factors were responsible for a decline in the number of young men in the relevant peak offending age ranges (10-14, 15-19 and 20-24 years) of almost 1 million (see Figure 17). These demographic developments clearly account for part of the decline in reported property offences during the Lawson boom; conversely, the upsurge in recorded property offences during the Major recession bucked these demographic developments. However, favourable demographics are not the whole story during the Lawson boom. Age-specific rates of cautionings and guilty findings for the age groups 14-17 and 17-21 for burglary are also sensitive to the business cycle (see Figure 18)

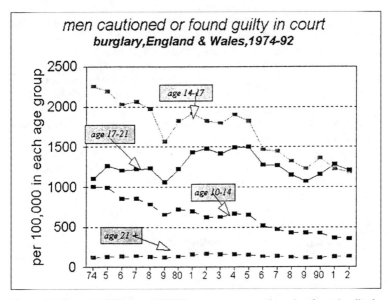

Figure 18: England & Wales, 1974-92: young men cautioned or found guilty in court for burglary (per 100,000 in each age group)

— and declined sharply during the Lawson boom.[30] If information on cautions and guilty findings can be used to draw inferences concerning underlying offending behaviour, the sharp decline in property crime during the Lawson boom can be ascribed to both a fall in offending and favourable demographics.

Data issues: (iii) police recruitment over the course of the economic cycle

A further possible objection to the evidence for the sensitivity of recorded property crime to the economic cycle derives from the work of Carr-Hill and Stern (1979). Using cross-section data from police force areas, they estimate a simultaneous equation model in which the offending rate is affected by the probability of deterrence (and, hence, by the size of the police force), whilst, simultaneously, police numbers respond to the number of recorded offences. In their model, police numbers are partly determined by the unemployment rate, since recruitment to the police is argued to be easier, the higher the current level of unemployment.[31] The possibility must, therefore, be considered that the reason recorded property offences move counter to the economic cycle is that, during recessions, there are higher levels of recording of underlying crime due to above trend increases in police recruitment (reflecting slack labour market conditions), whilst during economic up-turns, rates of recording fall as a result of below-trend increases in police numbers (reflecting labour market tightening).

However, data on police numbers for both England & Wales and Scotland strongly contradict this suggestion for the period since 1970. Police strengths rose strongly during each of the years when recorded property crime fell or registered below trend growth: 1973, 1978-9 and 1988-9. The 1977 (local) peak in recorded crime was one of the few years in which police numbers *fell*. And, following the lean years for police recruitment during the early 1980s (when recorded crime rose strongly), the pick-up in police numbers at the end of the 1980s coincided with the decline in recorded crime during the Lawson boom. If anything, the data on police strengths suggest an alternative and contradictory hypothesis to that suggested above, namely: poor economic performance is associated with an intensification of pressures on public expenditure (either as cause and/or effect) with adverse repercussions for police recruitment; but, this is associated with an above, rather than below, trend increase in recorded crime — possibly because of a lower police profile in the community, reduced risk of detection etc. — in addition to economic factors.

Crime and the business cycle:
the labour market as transmission mechanism

The graphs presented above provide an extraordinarily wide-ranging and consistent picture of the sensitivity of property crime to the economic cycle. The obvious question which arises is: what is the nature of the mechanism responsible for this relationship? The obvious candidate is changes in labour market conditions, especially when the causes of property crime are considered. Individuals when they are in work have a reasonable chance of satisfying their basic material needs as well as any higher order material aspirations through legitimate activities.[32] However, joblessness leads certain individuals to seek illegitimate means of satisfying their material needs. Either absolute or relative deprivation can be invoked as motives for unlawful behaviour as well as factors such as: frustrated aspirations, boredom, anger etc.[33] — bearing in mind that, even when the general level of unemployment is high, there exist ample opportunities for property crime, given the generally high level of material possessions owned by the great majority of the population who remain in employment. It follows that when the general level of employment is high, most people are able — and, perhaps, as important, *expect* to be able — to satisfy their needs through lawful activity. Conversely, when work is difficult to come by, large numbers of individuals are failing to meet their material needs, despite the social benefit system in place; and, just as important, have no *expectation* of being able to satisfy their needs legitimately. The blatant injustice of mass unemployment and enhanced inequality may then act to loosen ethical and moral constraints on unlawful behaviour — both at the level of the individual and, more importantly, when several unemployed individuals associate together. What evidence is there that changes in labour market conditions are the transmission mechanism responsible for the sensitivity of property crime to the economic cycle?

Field (1990a), having done so much to establish the sensitivity of property crime to the economic cycle, has generated considerable controversy by rejecting unemployment as a determinant of property crime in favour of changes in per capita private consumption. This conclusion is reached largely on statistical grounds as follows.

In order to model econometrically the relationship between crime and business fluctuations, the latter could, in principle, be represented statistically in various possible ways: for example, by changes in macro-economic variables, such as GDP, consumption and investment or by changes in labour market variables, such as employment, unemployment or labour force participation rates; one could even opt for an index of business sentiment. In Field's econometric work, changes in private consumption per head perform better statistically in accounting for changes in property crime; the coefficient on consumption changes is of the right sign (negative) and is significantly different statistically from zero — with consumption changes accounting for a high proportion of the variation in property crime. Unemployment, on the other hand, when it stands on its own is barely statistically significant and, when used in conjunction with consumption, adds little additional explanatory power.[34] Field (1990a) summarizes his results as follows. *'The analysis conducted here demonstrates an extremely strong relationship between crime and the business cycle, and demonstrates that unemployment adds nothing to the explanation of this pattern, once consumption growth — the key factor — is taken into account'*. This conclusion has been used by ministers in the present government to support their dismissal of a causal link running from unemployment to crime.[35,36]

A critique of Field

A simple single variable specification of the consumption-crime relationship confirms that year-to-year changes in real consumption per head are of the correct sign (negative) and a statistically significant determinant of year-to-year variations in property crime for England & Wales during 1970-92[37] and account for a very high 65% the total variation in property crime (see Appendix, equation 1) — although consumption is not at all significant for the preceding period 1950-69.[38] However, changes in real GDP per head, which is an alternative means (from the output side) of representing fluctuations in business activity, is also of the anticipated sign (negative) and statistically significant in a simple single variable specification — albeit accounting for slightly less (48%) of the year-to-year variation in property crime between 1970-92 (see Appendix, equation 2). That GDP and consumption are both statistically significant and have a high degree of explanatory power in relation to property crime confirms the sensitivity of property crime to the economic cycle. Both private consumption and GDP are well-recognized as *coincident* indicators of business activity and are highly correlated one with the other — consumption expenditure accounting for some 75% of GDP.

Unemployment, however, is well-recognized as a *lagging* indicator of economic activity. It should not be surprising, therefore, having already identified from our previous graphical work the sensitivity of property crime to the economic cycle, that unemployment should perform badly in correlation analysis. In fact, in a simple single variable specification, year-to-year changes in the official unemployment measure,[39] though of the right sign (positive) are barely statistically significant as a correlate of year-to-year variations in property crime and explain only 18% of the variation in the latter for England & Wales, 1970-92 (see Appendix — equation 3).

A good example of the way measured unemployment has, hitherto, lagged the economic cycle, thereby accounting for the poor regression result, can be taken from the recovery of the early 1980s: GDP turned up in 1981, employment began to increase in 1983, but the turning-point in claimant unemployment did not come until 1986.[40] It should not be surprising, therefore, that the sensitivity of property crime to the business cycle, as demonstrated by the graphs, will not be captured very well statistically by officially-measured unemployment.

The reason unemployment is a *lagging* indicator is generally thought to arise from both institutional and behaviourial factors. The existence of certain costs associated with both hiring and firing workers causes employers to treat labour somewhat as a fixed rather than a variable cost. As result, the actual labour force is only adjusted slowly to its desired size, for a given level of output, at each stage of the cycle — resulting in a tendency to hoard labour during the onset of recession (causing labour productivity growth to sag) and a reluctance to hire as recovery gets underway (when productivity growth soars). Compounding the effect of these lags in adjusting the actual to the desired labour force is the uncertainty which inevitably arises at turning-points in the cycle regarding the persistence or strength of the change in business conditions. The problem is compounded by shortcomings in the official 'claimant' count of the unemployed — which fails to include the non-claimant unemployed and those who respond to deteriorating employment conditions by withdrawing from the labour market.

The failure of statistical work using officially measured unemployment to capture the crime-business cycle relationship is no reason to reject the proposition that changes in labour market conditions are the transmission mechanism linking the business cycle with crime, because, although not conveyed by official unemployment statistics, labour market conditions almost certainly respond quite quickly to changed business conditions. As recession gets underway, firms are likely to respond to slack demand by cutting the length of the working-week and even hourly pay and by reducing new hirings; even if this change in labour market conditions does not show up as much, if any, of an increase in officially-measured unemployment, it may be reflected in a rise in the unregistered unemployed or in reduced labour force participation as workers are discouraged from seeking work. Conversely, as recovery gets underway, the new jobs which are created are partly filled by the unregistered unemployed and new entrants to the labour force and only partly, if at all, by people from off the claimant count.

Thus, the tendency for measured unemployment to lag the business cycle should not be taken to imply that labour market conditions are immune to turning-points in economic activity. Rather that our existing battery of statistical indicators is not adequate to the purpose in hand[41] — particularly as regards our measurement of the unregistered unemployed, changed participation rates etc.

Employment is known to be less of a lagging indicator than unemployment. And, in fact, it performs quite well as an explanatory variable in relation to property crime: the correct sign (negative) and statistically significantly different from zero during 1971-92,[42] it explains 34% of year-to-year variations in crime (see Appendix, equation (4)) — only slightly less than in the case of GDP per head. This suggests that, if it were possible to develop a labour market variable[43] which was sufficiently sensitive to changing labour market circumstances, it could perform at least as well as consumption per head.

Thus, even from a purely statistical point of view, we cannot dismiss changes in labour market conditions as the transmission mechanism responsible for the crime-business cycle link.

Moreover, from a *theoretical* perspective, the principal way in which consumption changes could impinge on crime is *through* changes in labour market conditions. This is recognized by Field (1990a) whose theoretical model explaining how changes in consumption are supposed to influence crime depends on labour market and unemployment effects. '*Potential offenders are likely to be concentrated in particular social groups, whose position in the labour market is liable to be weak or marginal. Fluctuations in aggregate consumption growth will therefore tend to be amplified in the experience of potential offenders, since marginal labour market groups commonly experience aggregate fluctuations in such an amplified form . . . It follows that a surge in consumption growth will be amplified in the experience of potential offenders . . . property crime will be lower than otherwise*' (p.6). Field's *theoretical* model appears to be sharply at odds with his strongly-drawn conclusions regarding the comparative lack of importance of unemployment as a causal factor in property crime. However, his policy prescriptions are at least consistent with the theory: *attempts to reduce the level of crime could usefully address the economic circumstances of those perceived to be at risk of criminal involvement'* (Field (1990b) p.9). What better way — indeed the only durable way — of improving the economic lot of such individuals than by generating higher levels of employment?

In view of this, it is something of a mystery that Field's work could have been used to discredit the hypothesis of a causal link running from unemployment to property crime.

Crimes of violence against the person and the business cycle

It is worth noting what Field discovered with regard to the link between unemployment and crimes of violence against the person. Unlike property crime, violent crimes against the person (of which minor assaults or 'punch-ups' are numerically the most important) appear to behave pro-cyclically. During up-swings in economic activity, young men have more money in their pockets, they go out and have a drink (or, more likely, several drinks) and they get into fights. During recessions, by contrast, money is tight, young men have less opportunity to go out and get drunk and, in consequence, there are fewer assaults. So, in the case of crimes of violence against the person, we have Field's 'consumption effect' depending on changes in labour market conditions — but, unlike property crime, behaving pro-cyclically. Interestingly, Field also finds a strong association between growth in offences of violence against the person and growth in unemployment during the previous year: *'These results strongly suggest that unemployment, and the relative deprivation associated with it, are conducive to violent crime. Given the lag between the growth in unemployment and violent crime, the relevant factor may be long-term unemployment'.*[44]

Further evidence: cross-section for 41 police areas — property crime and claimant unemployment

Despite the failure to detect much of a statistical relationship linking property crime and unemployment using time-series data, this is not the case when cross-section data are used. For 41 of the 42 police areas of England & Wales, data can be assembled on both recorded offences per 100,000 population and also claimant unemployment rates.[45,46]

In a simple single variable regression analysis, claimant unemployment is the correct sign (positive) and a statistically significant explanatory variable in the case of: residential burglary (accounting for 29% of the variation in the latter), theft of motor vehicles (31%), other theft (17%), robbery (23%) and burglary plus theft (23%) (see Appendix 1, equations (5)-(9)). Figures 19-22 contain scatter diagrams of the joint observations on each of these property crimes and claimant unemployment for the 41 police force areas in England & Wales in 1992 — together with the best fit regression line (statistically significant in each case).[47]

Despite the obvious simple-mindedness of the approach, the scatter diagrams suggest a strong association between crime and unemployment. The fact is: unemployment black spots in the country (Cleveland, Merseyside, Northumbria, Greater Manchester, South Yorkshire, West Midlands, Greater London, South Wales) are also crime black spots when it comes to the specific property crimes enumerated here. Of course, there exists considerable variation around the line of best fit; thus, West Yorkshire with claimant unemployment of just 9.0% has the highest recorded household burglary rate in the country: 2,483 per 100,000 population.[48] It is

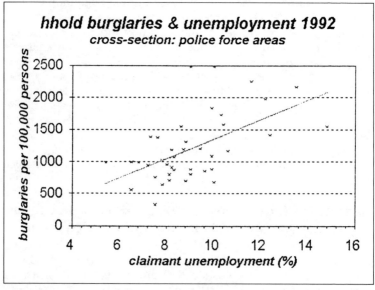

Figure 19: England & Wales 41 police areas: cross-section of household burglary (per 100,000 population) and claimant unemployment (%): scatter and best fit regression line

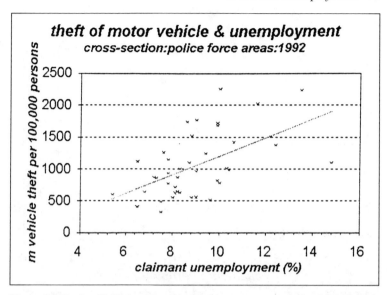

Figure 20: England & Wales 41 police force areas: cross-section of theft from motor vehicle (per 100,000 population) and claimant unemployment (%): scatter and best fit regression line

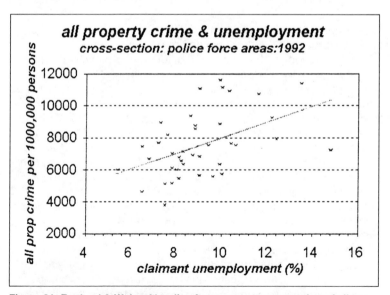

Figure 21: England & Wales 41 police force areas: cross-section of all property crime (per 100,000 population) and claimant unemployment (%): scatter and best fit regression line

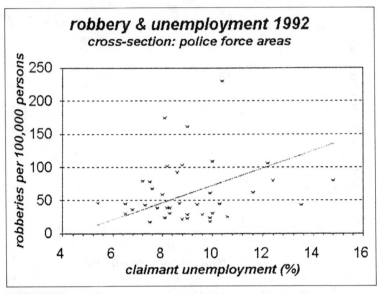

Figure 22: England & Wales 41 police force areas: cross-section of robbery (per 100,000 population) and claimant unemployment (%): scatter and best fit regression line

not being suggested, therefore, that this simple single variable model captures all the determinants of property crime.

One objection to this result is that unemployment is correlated with a great many other factors (e.g. poor housing, low educational attainment, poverty) which may act independently or interact with unemployment in causing crime: trying to identify the specific contribution of unemployment is, therefore, very difficult. Moreover, *'unemployment (given its inter-relationship with other economic and social factors) may be acting as a general measure of deprivation in an area which, rather than unemployment per se, is connected with crime'* (Tarling (1982)). However, it has to be said that, at the root of all these manifestations of social and economic deprivation lies poor regional/national economic performance, and the way this impinges on the lives of ordinary people is through depressed labour market conditions. Given vibrant local economies and high employment levels, poor housing, poverty and low educational attainments are all more amenable to improvement. That our great industrial conurbations and inner city areas are the nation's crime black spots must surely reflect the rapid de-industrialization of their employment structures which they have undergone during the past quarter century.

The cross-section results presented above are far from being the first work of this kind for Britain.[49] Stevens and Willis (1979) analyzed 1975 data for the divisions of the Metropolitan Police District and found white unemployment rates strongly correlated with white arrest rates across the boroughs of London.[50] Timbrell (1988) estimates a cross-section model in which the following are tested for as determinants of property crime: the level of economic welfare,[51] educational attainment, age composition (to pick up the contribution of young men to crime, noted earlier) and unemployment. When both the welfare/wealth and unemployment variables are included in the regression analysis, the former is statistically significant and the latter not — causing the author to conclude that: *'there is clear evidence that the crime rate is greatly affected (largely determined) by the economic welfare of the population. More wealth means less crime ... but none that unemployment is an independent factor in determining crime'* (p.26). This conclusion is not, however, supported by the research. Wealth/welfare (as measured by the number of cars per household) is, as might be expected, highly correlated with unemployment on a cross-section basis between the counties of England & Wales; when wealth is omitted from the equation, unemployment is statistically significant as a determinant of household burglary and explains a high degree of variance in the latter. This suggests the strength or weakness of the local/regional economy is a determinant of crime levels. Such strength/weakness has many manifestations; but the main way in which it impinges on the life of ordinary people is through the vibrancy or otherwise of the local labour market. Hence, it is reasonable to propose the labour market as the transmission mechanism linking the business cycle with property crime.

Further evidence: crime and unemployment — changes between police force areas over time

An even more demanding test of the statistical association between crime and unemployment is to see whether, looking across the police districts of England & Wales, increases in offences over time are correlated with increases in unemployment. We examine increases in crime[52] between 1975 and 1992 (both recession years but the number unemployed nationally in 1992 was three times higher than in 1975).[53] In simple regressions of the increase in the offence rate (for household burglary and motor vehicle theft, respectively)[54] on the increase in unemployment between 1975-92 by police force area, unemployment is the correct sign (positive) and statistically significant in both cases: accounting for 24% of the variation in household burglary increases and 13% in the case of motor vehicle theft.[55] Figures 23 and 24 contain scatters of changes in household burglary and motor vehicle theft, respectively, and changes in unemployment for each of 41 police force areas and the best fit regression line. Whilst the degree of explanation of the statistical variation is relatively small, it must be appreciated that this is a quite demanding test of the crime-unemployment hypothesis.

Crime and long-term unemployment

As a preliminary to studying the links between long-term unemployment and crime, we begin with a brief statistical overview of long-term unemployment. The normal convention is to define the long-term unemployed as those unemployed for one year or more — and we follow this convention, although some people regard being unemployed for 6 months or more as constituting long-term unemployment.

Despite the change to the *Labour Force Survey* definition of unemployment between 1983/4,[56] the *LFS* is a better source of

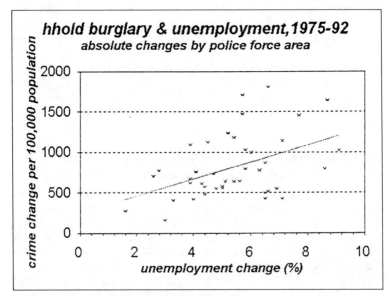

Figure 23: England & Wales 41 police force areas: changes in household burglary *versus* changes in claimant unemployment between 1975 and 1992: scatter and best fit regression line

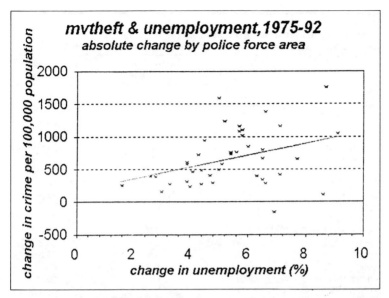

Figure 24: England & Wales 41 police force areas: changes in motor vehicle theft *versus* changes in claimant unemployment between 1975 and 1992: scatter and best fit regression line

information about unemployment in general and long-term unemployment in particular than the monthly claimant count because the latter has been subject to so many changes of both administrative and statistical kinds — particularly with respect to the enumeration of the long-term unemployed. To give only the most obvious example: men aged 60 and over who are on income support following the exhaustion of their entitlement to national insurance unemployment benefit after 12 months on the dole are no longer (following rule changes in 1982/3) required to 'sign on' to obtain benefit. This introduced a major discontinuity into the series on long-term unemployment derived from the monthly claimant count (see Table 1).[57]

Several aspects of these series on long-term unemployment are worthy of comment.

First, the numbers of long-term unemployed, which were negligible in the 1950s and 1960s era of full employment, rose rapidly during the 1970s as the economy departed from full employment to stand at 300 thousand by the end of the 1970s. Long-term unemployment then rose by a million to stand at over 1.3 million in the mid-1980s. The Lawson boom resulted in a halving of the numbers of long-term unemployed — which shows that

Table 1
Long-term unemployment from the *Labour Force Survey*
Great Britain; men & women; not seasonally-adjusted, thousands

Date	Total unemployed	Unemployed > 1 year	% unemployed > 1 year
1965	362	60	16.6
1970	609	97	16.0
Spring 1977	1456	382	26.2
Spring 1979	1271	312	24.5
Spring 1981	2447	636	24.5
Spring 1983	2910	1301	44.7
Spring 1984	2905	1329	45.7
Spring 1985	2814	1264	44.9
Spring 1986	2969	1155	38.9
Spring 1987	2879	1115	38.7
Spring 1988	2376	1014	42.7
Spring 1989	1978	756	38.2
Spring 1990	1869	631	33.8
Spring 1991	2302	655	28.5
Spring 1992	n.a.	n.a.	n.a.
Winter 1992/93	2920	1168	40.0
Spring 1993	2804	1181	42.1
Summer 1993	2894	1179	40.7
Autumn 1993	2792	1211	43.4
Winter 1993/94	2737	1196	43.7
Spring 1994	2615	1170	44.7
Summer 1994	2679	1126	42.0

Source: for 1965 and 1970, DE, *Gazette*; subsequently: *Labour Force Surveys*
(various).

several years of high tempo economic growth[58] can make striking erosions into even long-term unemployment. However, with the onset of the 1990s recession, long-term unemployment has risen to levels not far short of those of the mid-1980s — despite numerous Employment Service measures (including Re-start) targeted specifically at the long-term unemployed.

Second, long-term unemployment exhibits much greater volatility than total unemployment — with the share of the long-term unemployed rising when total unemployment increases and falling when total unemployment declines. Two reasons can be advanced why the share of the long-term unemployed rises during recessions. During an economic downturn, inflows into unemployment exceed outflows and people are, therefore, more likely to get stuck on the register and slip over into longer duration spells of unemployment. Furthermore, the probability of getting a job and ceasing to be unemployed declines with duration, reflecting the fact that what jobs are available go to those with shorter-duration spells. However,

Table 2
Long-term unemployment from the *Labour Force Survey*
Great Britain: Men & Women separately,[1] not seasonally-adjusted, thousands

Date	Men			Women		
	Total un-employed	> 1 year*	%*	Total un-employed	> 1 year*	%*
1965	274	52	19.0	88	8	9.1
1970	523	89	17.0	85	8	9.7
Spring 1979	590	197	33.4	302	66	21.8
Spring 1981	1391	437	31.4	597	145	24.3
Spring 1983	1876	954	52.3	1027	357	36.0
Spring 1984	1813	958	55.0	1094	379	36.4
Spring 1985	1903	917	55.2	1248	353	36.0
Spring 1986	1919	879	52.3	1254	324	32.7
Spring 1987	1847	856	52.9	1226	308	32.1
Spring 1988	1509	787	54.3	1031	577	29.2
Spring 1989	1247	577	48.6	879	231	28.1
Spring 1990	1187	480	40.7	821	187	22.9
Spring 1991	1536	492	32.2	915	192	21.1
Spring 1992	n.a.	n.a.	n.a.	n.a.	n.a.	n.a.
Winter 1992/3	1981	880	44.4	939	288	30.6
Spring 1993	1904	887	46.6	900	294	32.7
Summer 1993	1923	887	46.1	971	293	30.1
Autumn 1993	1838	910	49.5	954	301	31.5
Winter 1993/4	1833	908	49.5	904	289	31.9
Spring 1994	1747	887	50.8	867	271	30.7
Summer 1994	1795	855	47.6	883	271	30.7

Source: 1965 and 1970: DE, *Gazette*; up to Spring 1992: Eurostat, *Labour Force Survey* and from Winter 1992/3 onwards DE, *Labour Force Survey: Quarterly Bulletin*.
[1] These figures do not necessarily sum to those for men and women together given in Table 1 in the case of *Eurostat* data.
*The number unemployed for 1 year or more and the equivalent % only refer in the case of *Eurostat* data to those for whom duration data were available and are not therefore consistent with the total unemployed figure.

it is significant that a period of sustained economic gorwth will result in a decline in the share of the long-term unemployed in the total — despite the fact that probability of exiting unemployment declines the longer the duration.

A third point is that, regionally, unemployment durations are longer, the higher is the overall level of unemployment. And in regions with above-average unemployment rates, the probability of exiting from the register is lower for every duration and, hence, the chance of becoming long-term unemployed is higher.

Other statistical characteristics of the long-term unemployed (derived from the *Eurostat* compilation of the *Labour Force Survey* results for EU member states) (see Table 2) are: (i) amongst unemployed men, almost half are long-term unemployed — a figure some two-thirds higher than for women;[59] (ii) the share of long-term in total unemployment was higher in GB than the EU average in the mid-1980s — but was lower in 1990-1 following the Lawson boom and Employment Service measures targeted on the long-term unemployed.

Finally, despite long-term unemployment exhibiting greater cyclical fluctuations than total unemployment, there is some evidence that, at the turning-points in the business cycle, long-term unemployment lags changes in economic activity by even more than total unemployment. Thus, during the early stages of the 1990s recession, long-term unemployment rose less fast than total unemployment (and, hence, declined as a share of the total). Symmetrically, during the current output recovery, much of the reduction in unemployment has been concentrated in the shorter durations (this is so whether the *Labour Force Survey* or claimant definitions of unemployment are used), with the result that the numbers of long-term unemployed have only shown a sustained fall since April 1994[60] — more than a year after the turn-down in claimant unemployment — with a consequential rise in the long-term unemployed share during the initial stages of recovery (see Table 2).

It is reasonably obvious why long-term unemployment should be more of a lagging indicator than total unemployment. During the early stages of recessions, increased inflows onto the register of the newly-unemployed increase the share of short-duration unemployment in total, and it takes time for the newly-unemployed to move into the higher duration categories — although durations of the existing unemployed will increase as outflows from unemployment decline. Equally, during the early stages of recovery, the long-term unemployed are likely to be handicapped in competing for available jobs compared with both short-duration unemployed and new labour force entrants because of either real or perceived disadvantages accruing from a long spell of joblessness.

The fact that long-term unemployment is even more of a lagging indicator than unemployment itself means that, in attempting to uncover the transmission mechanism responsible for the sensitivity of property crime to the business cycle, long-term unemployment is not going to show up as a statistically significant determinant of property crime.

This in no way means, however, that long-term unemployment is not an important causal factor in determining crime. It seems very plausible that prolonged individual spells of unemployment , particularly where spatially concentrated, are likely to prove a fertile breeding-ground for crime. In addition to the usual motivating factors (absolute and relative deprivation and thwarted ambition),[61] long-duration unemployment, which possibly stretches from one generation to the next, casts a cloud over the whole community. As Box (1987) argues strongly, it undermines the family and, therefore, weakens the social bonds which contribute to ensuring lawful behaviour. The absence of future employment prospects de-legitimizes school and results in many pupils becoming cynical, bored and rebellious. The future no longer holds out the prospect of material and social success, and so young people see no point in making a 'stake in conformity'. Unemployment *'affects individual beliefs in the legitimacy of conformity to conventional rules and norms because, having undermined the stability of the family and the relevance of schools, both major instruments for socialization, it damages the ability of one generation to imprint its values on the next'* (Box (1987), p.45).

Other aggregate studies
linking crime and unemployment

It is well-established that young men are responsible for a disproportionate share of crime. Males between the ages of 17 and 25 constituted 69.7% of total adult convictions and cautions and 48.5% of all convictions and cautions for burglary committed in 1990; whilst cautioning and conviction rates for burglaries for males under 25 were between six and eight times higher than males aged over 25. Concerned by this and by the possible shortcomings of studies using highly aggregate data, my colleague, David Dickinson, has analyzed the relationship between conviction rates for burglary amongst young males and unemployment amongst the same group during the past two decades (Dickinson (1994)). In the past couple of decades, unemployment rates amongst young adult males[62] have been at levels slightly more than twice that of adult males as a whole. Dickinson's results can be summarized as follows: (i) burglary conviction and caution rates for men under 25 closely follow the economic cycle — with the offence rate declining during years of recovery: 1973 (Barber boom), 1978 and 1979 (post-OPEC recovery) and 1986-87-88-89 (Lawson boom) as well as 1974 and 1990; (ii) the offence rate is correlated with the unemployment rate for this group — though the offence rate is shifting up over time for a given unemployment rate; (iii) in a regression analysis of annual changes in the offence rate on annual changes in the unemployment rate for this group, unemployment is statistically significant and accounts for 40% of the year-to-year variation in offences.

The exceptionally high age specific offence rates for young men confirm the well-known observation that the transition from adolescence to adulthood is fraught with difficulties. The exceptionally high unemployment rates experienced by young people must surely serve to make this transition more difficult. Admittedly, high youth unemployment rates to some degree reflect experimentation ('chopping & changing') by young people with respect to both different employers and different possible occupations; average unemployment durations are shorter for the young than for the older unemployed so, on this account, their unemployment appears to constitute less of a problem. However, given the high proclivity of this group to criminal activity, society is taking a great risk in running such high unemployment rates amongst such a sensitive group. As David Dickinson comments: 'By allowing mass unemployment to continue, and letting young men shoulder a disproportionate burden of this, we condemn ourselves to rising crime now and (given the high recidivism rates) create criminals for the future'.

Brief review of some disaggregated/micro studies (of individuals) on the crime-unemployment link[63]

Writing in 1982, Roger Tarling reported that 'research studies of known offenders had repeatedly shown that somewhere in the region of four out of ten were unemployed; a much higher proportion than the population as a whole'. But this proportion has almost certainly risen during the period of much higher unemployment witnessed during the 1980s. Tarling is somewhat dismissive of such evidence as indicative of a causal relationship from unemployment to crime on the grounds that: (i) many offences are committed by individuals still in full-time education; (ii) causality may run in the opposite direction: having a criminal record may exacerbate employment problems and (iii) some offenders may choose to be unemployed as a way of life. On point (i), the evidence reviewed below indicates that family economic and social deprivation are important precursors of juvenile (in school) delinquency. On point (ii), though convicted offenders certainly find it more difficult to get a job, it is clear that the emergence of mass unemployment in the UK reflects poor economic performance not the rise in crime!

The Cambridge Institute of Criminology's longitudinal study of predominantly white, inner city males born in 1953 throws light on the link between unemployment and young adult criminality in the period between leaving school in 1967/8 and 1971/2. Since this was a period of relatively full employment, this study does not purport to measure the impact of prolonged mass unemployment nor long-term unemployment. Nevertheless, the results seem clear enough. The rate of offending was about three times as great for individuals experiencing unemployment as for those with work (0.49 offences per year compared with 0.16). Moreover, the frequency of offences rose for those youths who had experienced longer periods of unemployment (three months or more). Offenders were twice as likely to commit crimes of material gain during unemployment than when employed (0.83 offences per year compared with 0.39) — though they were almost equally likely to commit offences other than those for material gain while unemployed or employed (0.36 offences per year compared with 0.38).

Interestingly, the study found that, when combined with a method of predicting delinquency at the age of 10,[64] the rate of offending only increased during unemployment for those with scores of 5 or more out of 7 (2.5 offences per year compared with 1.02). The authors therefore concluded that while young people are more likely to commit crimes when they are unemployed and that it may, therefore, be regarded as having a criminogenic effect, unemployment does not seem to cause 'basically law-abiding youths to commit crimes'. But, the results indicate that those most at risk of engaging in offending behaviour as a result of a disadvantaged background have their propensity to commit crime enhanced by unemployment.

A further study by Gormally *et al* (1991) surveyed 123 offenders referred to the probation services between the ages of 16 and 18 in Northern Ireland during 1980. The aim of the survey was to see if offenders of this age group had a higher unemployment rate than that of non-offenders. The unemployment rate for the surveyed group at the time of offending was found to be 68% — far higher than that of young people in general. Moreover, the periods in which the offenders had not committed crimes, 'straight periods', were found to be longer when they contained some experience of full-time employment (10.2 months compared to 6.0 months for periods without this experience). The average duration of straight periods was also higher for those who had any experience of full-time work (irrespective of whether it occurred during that particular straight period) than for those who had no such experience (8.5 months compared with 5.1 months).

The report found that the majority of young people surveyed suffered from multiple disadvantages, apart from low employment, but concluded that unemployment *'has a separate effect on the likelihood of individuals committing offences'*.

Crime and unemployment:
from data to theory and policy

Arguing that labour market conditions are an important causal factor in determining property crime does not imply that all individuals who become unemployed then go out and commit crime. That is patently untrue. Unemployment does not necessarily lead otherwise law-abiding individuals into criminal behaviour — although it might do. Moreover, certain offences are committed by people who not only have a job — but whilst they are actually at their place of work. And many crimes are committed by young people before they even enter the labour market — for many years, the peak rate of 'known' offending (including cautions) by age amongst men was one year below the minimum school-leaving age (Barclay (1990)) and is now between 17 and 18, though for women it is between 14 and 15. Nor do any but a tiny minority of those advocating that unemployment is causally related to crime believe that it is the only factor such that, were there to be a return to full employment, we could expect to see property crime vanish. Unemployment is just one factor in a complex set of determinants.

However, given the aggregate statistical evidence presented here as well as the resulst of micro studies, unemployment can surely not be ignored/rejected as a causal factor. Having presented the empirical evidence, it is necessary to theorize how unemployment could affect crime.

There are a number of ways in which unemployment is likely to impact on property crime. First, there is the purely material aspect of becoming unemployed and poor in what is still a very wealthy society. Unemployment results in a considerable reduction in material living-standards (Garman *et al* (1991)) and, even with current welfare provision, can result in severe material deprivation. The gap which opens up between people's basic material needs — let alone their aspirations for goods and services addressing higher level needs — and the legal possibilities for satisfying them must place pressure on those individuals to turn to criminal activity to meet their needs. At the same time, even when claimant unemployment has risen to levels of 3 million and above, the vast majority of the population remain in work and enjoy not only a high material standard-of-living but also high levels of ownership of material possessions — thereby, presenting opportunities for gain through criminal activity. Such possibilities must have been enhanced by the very rapid growth during the past decade in the incomes of those already at the top of the income pyramid who must surely be a tempting target for those who have little legal claim on society's resources.[65] Thus, the juxtaposition of being unemployed and poor in what is basically a very wealthy society must inevitably create tensions and give rise to feelings of anger, envy and resentment — the more so as the means by which some of the high incomes have accrued during the past decade (in the City, the privatized utilities etc.) lack social legitimacy, not only amongst the poor and unemployed as well as throughout society more generally.

The impoverishing effect of unemployment on the propensity to commit crime must surely have been accentuated by the rise in recent years of acquisitive individualism; namely, the marrying together of the materialistic ethic (portraying the acquisition of material goods and services as the high road to human happiness) with an individualism which is sometimes asserted at the expense of fellow members of society. Lacking the legal means to acquire the appurtances of a consumer society must be especially galling in a society which places so much stress on the benefits accruing from material possessions, whilst the 'get rich quick, let the devil take the hindmost' philosophy which has flourished in recent years provides a convenient cover, were one to be required, for criminal behaviour. That the means by which some of the high incomes in society have been generated seem little more than legalized robbery (in monopoly privatized utilities, the quangocracy, financial speculation etc.) cannot have helped.

Moreover, the unemployed suffer not merely material deprivation; they are also denied all the satisfactions which work is increasingly recognized as bringing to the individual. For many of those in employment, work is obviously a feature of central importance in their lives: not just because it occupies a large proportion of their waking hours but also because of the challenges which it brings, both mental and manual; the fact that work also provides many individuals with an important part of their sense of identity and a feeling of contributing something to society; the financial independence from the state together with the satisfactions from social contacts work brings are also important. Unemployment, particularly a prolonged spell of joblessness, by depriving an individual of these benefits, must inevitably give rise to anger. In some individuals, such anger will be directed inwards resulting in loss of self-esteem, feelings of worthlessness, impotence and depression; in others, such angry feelings will be directed outwards at the rest of society — taking, for some, the constructive form of, say, political action, whilst others will turn to crime.[66]

Finally, mass unemployment on the scale which the UK has experienced since the late 1970s and increasing relative inequality in income and wealth must surely lead to an erosion of individual moral constraint on unlawful behaviour — not necessarily confined to the unemployed themselves but spread more widely in the community, particularly where unemployment and long-term unemployment are spatially concentrated. Mass unemployment constitutes the breakdown of an implicit social contract and set of mutual responsibilities between the governing classes and the governed. The gradual emergence of a situation in which large numbers of people in a completely urban setting find themselves without gainful employment represents nothing less than a very considerable act of cruelty visited on those people. In a rural or semi-industrialized society, unemployment resulting from the loss of wage employment is made half-bearable by the existence of multifarious alternatives for deploying one's time and eking out a livelihood. But, with the advent of industrial capitalism, concentrating millions of people into large urban conurbations, society implicitly acquired a duty to provide gainful employment to its urban denizens. This implicit social contract (made explicit by the 1944 White Paper) having self-evidently broken down with the emergence of mass unemployment in recent years must act as a solvent on individual moral constraints on unlawful behaviour, because such constraints, though partly inherent and taught, also depend on the legitimacy and acceptability of the social and economic order. An advanced industrial system that operates permanently under conditions of mass unemployment risks losing legitimacy and acceptability amongst large numbers of its citizens — the more so if the members of the ruling elite appear to enjoy huge financial rewards which cannot be related to their productivity. The rising tide of crime and delinquency must owe something to the break-down of this social compact, to a growing sense of unfairness and to the stifling of potential represented by unemployment.

These ideas also need to be linked to our knowledge of the precursors of delinquent behaviour derived from longitudinal surveys such as the Cambridge Institute of Criminology's study of about 400 predominantly white inner city males born in 1953 (Farrington (1988)). This study identifies the following factors at age 8-10 as significantly predicting convicted as opposed to unconvicted men and chronic as opposed to non-chronic offenders: (i) economic deprivation, including low income, poor housing, unemployment spells experienced by parents; (ii) family criminality, including convicted parents and delinquent siblings; (iii) unsatisfactory parenting (too authoritarian or too unbounded); (iv) school failure — often reflecting behaviourial disorders such as hyperactivity, impulsivity etc. Even these apparently non-economic factors could have their origins in material deprivation. A key predictor of persistent offending at age 14-18 was being unemployed at age 16, whilst, of late-comers to crime during their twenties, the only statistically significant predictor was unemployment at age 18. The principal policy recommendations of the authors were: *'There should be a determined effort to reduce crime by social prevention . . . the worst offenders were drawn from the poorest families in the worst housing . . . more resources should be targeted selectively on the poorest families to try to improve their economic circumstances . . . If it is true that 5% of the population commits 50% of all crime (or some similar disproportionality), it may be more economical to target 5% of the people rather than 50% of the crimes'.*

The empirical evidence which informed these conclusions was obtained during a period of relatively full employment. However, it is unlikely that the basic precursors of crime should have changed under the impact of mass unemployment — if anything, they have been reinforced. Conditions of mass unemployment and other social changes such as the growth of single parenthood have brought with them poverty on a scale not witnessed since the 1930s — with now 1 in 4 children being from families in receipt of Income Support. The message from the Cambridge longitudinal survey is that a society with such large numbers of families and children in poverty runs the risk of massive criminal delinquency. A return to much higher levels of employment represents the best way of addressing such poverty.

Conclusions

If we are going to be 'tough on crime and tough on the causes of crime', then we have to come down very hard on two of the well-documented causes of crime: unemployment and poverty.

Footnotes
1. Faculty of Economics, University of Cambridge.
2. Data for Scotland are published in the Scottish Office publication *Statistical Bulletin: Criminal Justice Series.*
3. Undertaken in 1981, 1983, 1987, 1991 and 1992. The results of the first Scottish Crime Survey have recently been published; see Anderson and Leitch (1994).
4. The exceptions in the case of the household-based *BCS* are: shoplifting, fraud and commercial burglary (where the victim is a corporate entity) and household violence. See Mayhew *et al* (1993).
5. Estimates for 1991 computed as the product of the % of incidents reported and the % of reported incidents recorded by the police; see Mayhew *et al* (1993), Tables A2.5 and A2.6 pps.115 and 116.
6. Whilst violence against the person includes homicide, much the greater proportion consists of 'other woundings etc' i.e. punch-ups between youths.

7. Data are averages for England & Wales for 1993 from *Criminal Statistics: England & Wales Supplementary Tables 1993* Vol.3.

8. Although 56% of all household burglaries in 1992 involved value of property stolen of less than £50 and 71% costs of damage of less than £50; see Mayhew *et al* (1993), Table A4.9, p.124.

9. Deviations about the rising trend will be discussed in greater detail below.

10. Note that the recently-published *Scottish Crime Survey* for 1993 (Anderson and Leitch (1994)) reaches similar conclusions, namely: underlying or 'true' crime rose by just 5% between 1981 and 1992 as against an increase of 52% in police statistics of comparable recorded crime. However, estimates of housebreaking and other acquisitive crimes covered by the *SCS* have risen broadly in line with police statistics, but crimes involving violence have risen much more slowly and vandalism has declined.

11. *Criminal Statistics England & Wales 1992*, p.97. For many years, the peak rate of 'known' offending (including cautions) by age amongst men was one year below the minimum school-leaving age (Barclay (1990)) but has now risen to between 17 and 18; for women it is between 14 and 15.

12. See Farrington *et al* (1988).

13. Thus, the Cambridge Institute of Criminology longitudinal study of a cohort of about 400 predominantly white, inner city males born in 1953 shows the peak age range for self-reported offences to be 10-14 years (with an 88.6% offence rate) — though vandalism and petty fraud (mainly fare cheating) figured prominently in the crimes committed in this age range; see Farrington *et al* (1988).

14. These results confirm those of the Cambridge Institute of Criminology's longitudinal survey; see Farrington *et al* (1988).

15. Reilly and Witt (1992) combine both time-series and cross-section data in order to augment the volume of information.

16. Tarling (1982) writing in 1982 was surely premature to argue that 'aggregate studies . . . have probably exhausted their potential to illuminate a connection between unemployment and criminal behaviour'. Improvements in crime statistics (in particular, the regular appearance of the *BCS* providing a more accurate picture of both the trend and fluctuations in underlying offending behaviour), the emergence of mass unemployment (when a crime-unemployment relationship of a different kind from that which existed during the earlier full employment era may emerge) and the fact that the sensitivity of property crime to the business cycle has become particularly apparent since 1970 are all factors making for the continuing relevance of *aggregate* studies.

17. An excellent survey of the empirical evidence on both the crime-unemployment and crime-inequality relationship covering both UK and US experience can be found in Box (1987), Chapter 3. US evidence is surveyed in Freeman (1983).

18. See Field (1990), Table 3, p.2 — though this result can be criticized on the grounds of lack of comparability of all the statistical indicators employed over such a long time period. Field finds year-to-year changes in property crime more highly correlated with changes in per head consumption than unemployment (for a critical discussion, see text below).

19. Defined between 1950-68 as the sum of: larceny plus breaking and entering plus receiving plus frauds and false pretences (see *Criminal Statistics England & Wales 1970*, p.xxv). For 1969-93, property crimes defined as the sum of: all burglary (residential and commercial), all theft and handling of stolen goods, robbery and fraud and forgery. 'Criminal damage' (or vandalism), though a property crime, has been excluded both because of the small proportion of such offences which find their way into police records (1 in 7 in 1992 according to

the *BCS*) and the lack of an historically consistent series.

20. England & Wales and Scotland, with their differing legal systems, have slightly different definitions of the relevant crime categories, and in both official statistical publications and the plots presented in this note, data are presented separately.

21. The Scottish category of 'crimes of dishonesty' includes residential burglary, theft and fraud; see Scottish Office, *Statistical Bulletin* (Criminal Justice Series).

22. Although a number of other factors, independent of the state of the economy, have been adduced to explain the reduction in overall property crime observed in 1993, namely: members of the public taking increased security measures in reaction to the crime wave, the spread of household insurance policies with features such as 'no claims' bonuses and deductible amounts thereby reducing the reporting of crime to the police. Note also that not all categories of property crime decreased: non-residential burglary declined but residential burglary increased; theft from a motor vehicle fell but theft of a motor vehicle rose.

23. In a statistical regression relating year-to-year changes in property crime to changes in (separately) per cap GDP, per cap consumption and unemployment (taking first differences of the logs in each case) for the period 1950-69, the explanatory variables are not statistically significantly different from zero and the degree of explanation of variation in crime is low. There is no point in presenting the details of these nil results.

24. Phillips (1994).

25. See Carr-Hill and Stern (1979), p.271.

26. Increases in reporting being offset by a decrease in recording.

27. See Mayhew *et al* (1993), Figure 4.1, p.43.

28. *Criminal Statistics England & Wales 1992*, p.97.

29. See Farrington *et al* (1988), Table 4.1, p.77.

30. Note that age specific rates of cautioning plus guilty findings trend downwards for both juveniles and young adults but especially for the 10-14 age group. This appears to reflect a greater resort to warnings on the part of police — in light of the adverse 'labelling' effect of court appearances on young offenders.

31. See Carr-Hill and Stern (1979), p.75. Note that the authors drew their empirical evidence from the 1960s and 1970s, when near full employment conditions prevailed and the police's ability to recruit up to full establishment levels was frequently constrained by labour market tightness.

32. Though people with jobs certainly do commit offences; indeed, a certain amount of crime occurs at the workplace.

33. See Box (1987), Chapter 2, for an approach which attempts to integrate many different theories positing a crime-unemployment relationship.

34. Reilly and Witt (1992) make the important criticism that, if an attempt is being made to identify a variable representing the business cycle, then using *both* consumption and unemployment involves a redundancy. 'In modelling the relationship between the business cycle and crime, both variables can be viewed as proxying the same effect. It's not clear that there is gain in including both' (p.214).

35. Thereby ignoring Field's *caveat*: 'It does not follow that unemployment cannot cause crime. For a potential or actual offender, the experience of unemployment might precipitate offending or an increase in offending' (p.7).

36. Field attempts to explain the contradiction between his failure to identify the crime-unemployment relationship statistically at the aggregate level and his view that an unemployment spell may increase the likelihood of offending behaviour by referring to the possibility that unemployment amongst actual and potential offenders may diverge from the average picture. This is intrinsically implausible as unemployment rates for different age, sex, ethnic, and regional groups are all

highly correlated over time. In fact, unemployment rates amongst young males, who have the highest offending rates, exhibit a higher degree of variance than overall unemployment rates and may, possibly, be a leading indicator of overall unemployment.

37. Field's econometric work is much more sophisticated than the simple single variable specification whose results are reported below (see Appendix) — but this simple specification captures the essence of the issue. Following Field, first differences of the log of all the variables are employed in the time-series analysis.

38. Indicating either: (i) a structural shift in the relationship in 1970 or (ii) more likely: data problems, in particular, increased reporting prior to 1970 which undermine the quality of recorded crime data prior to 1970 — in particular, as regards the measurement of year-to-year changes.

39. Unemployment for England & Wales is measured for: (i) 1974-92 as claimant unemployed (extrapolated backwards on a basis consistent with the current coverage of the benefit regime) as % of the work-force; data from *Monthly Digest of Statistics* database and *Economic Trends Annual Supplement* and (ii) 1954-74 data on registered unemployed from *Regional Trends* computed as % of employees plus unemployed. The two series were linked on the claimant basis in 1974.

40. Although, during the current recovery, the fall in claimant unemployment (in January 1993) lagged the turning-point in GDP by just nine months.

41. The same point has recently been made by Pyle and Deadman (1994).

42. The slight shortening of time period reflects slightly reduced data availability for employment compared with other variables.

43. Further work is continuing on this topic.

44. Field (1990a), p.46.

45. The exception is Surrey which lacks claimant unemployment data. Police force areas mainly correspond to counties — though often with some aggregation (e.g. Thames Valley police force covers the counties of Berkshire, Buckinghamshire and Oxfordshire etc.).

46. The data sources are *Criminal Statistics England & Wales 1992* and *Employment Gazette*. Claimant unemployment rates for June 1992 were used.

47. Whereas the regression results are based on the logs of the variables, the scatters are of the untransformed values of the variables which are also those used to compute the best fit regression line plotted — for ease of understanding.

48. Note that claimant unemployment is a far from perfect index of local labour market conditions. For one thing, it excludes the non-claimant unemployed (estimated at 991,000 nationally in Winter 1993/4 from the *Labour Force Survey*) as well as claimant unemployed who have been allowed to 'sign off' as well as 'discouraged workers' i.e. those unemployed who have given up job search because they believe no jobs are available. Adjustment to poor employment prospects also takes the form of out-migration to more prosperous regions.

49. See Carr-Hill and Stern (1979), Box (1987) Table 3.2, p.85, who uses the same data source for a different year and Timbrell (1988).

50. Tarling (1982) questioned the obvious implication of this result for employment policy on the grounds that black and Asian arrest rates were not correlated with their own unemployment rates but with those of whites. However, since what prompted the study — and was the main focus of its analysis — was above-normal arrests rates for blacks, such an absence of correlation is, perhaps, not surprising. Differences in white unemployment rates may have been acting, Tarling argues, as an index of differential social deprivation between the London boroughs — but this should not call into question the causal role of poor economic and employment conditions in generating that deprivation.

51. Measured (obviously not satisfactorily) by the number of cars per household.
52. The absolute increase in the number of offences committed per 100,000 population is compared with the absolute increase in the % unemployed. The absolute increase is a better indicator than the % change: thus, a doubling in the rate of unemployment from 1% to 2% can be argued to be less damaging than a doubling from, say, 6% to 12%. The same applies to the offence rate data.
53. There are formidable data problems involved in undertaking this exercise affecting the comparability over time of both crime and unemployment data, which are more serious in the case of the latter than the former (there is a minor discontinuity affecting the crime series between 1979 and 1980). The frequently-revised claimant unemployment series consistent with the current coverage of the benefit regime is not available at the level of counties/police force areas for 1975. Thus, we have been forced to compare unadjusted registered unemployment for 1975 (November figure) with claimant unemployment for 1992 (June figure). UK registered unemployment in November 1975 was 1.125 million compared with 975.9 thousand for 4th quarter 1975 on a revised claimant basis. The denominator in the unemployment expression in both years has been the sum of unemployed plus employees in employment — the procedure adopted in the case of registered unemployment, thereby preserving at least some degree of comparability — though the denominator for claimant unemployment now includes, additionally, self-employed, HM Forces and trainees.
54. Examination of this relationship was restricted to these two offences (already shown by the 1992 cross-section for 1992 to be correlated with claimant unemployment) on account of a shortage of time.
55. The statistical fit would have been better in the case of motor vehicle theft but for the outlying observation for Merseyside. In 1975, Merseyside had the highest rate of motor vehicle theft per 100,000 population and the highest unemployment rate within our sample; however, by 1992, despite experiencing one of the larger increases in unemployment in the sample, motor vehicle theft actually declined — the only police force area in the country to have experienced this. This, perhaps, illustrates that prolonged adverse economic circumstances eventually constrain the level of offences by reducing the scope/opportunity for undertaking property-related crime.
56. The ILO definition of unemployment deployed from 1984 onwards refers to people without a job and who would like to work who were available to start work in the two weeks following their *LFS* interview and had either looked for work in the four weeks prior to interview or were waiting to start a job they had already obtained. The so-called *LFS* definition of unemployment used in earlier surveys was more restrictive on the job search side (1 week as against 4) but did not contain an availability condition. The ILO unemployment definition excludes 907,000 (as of Summer 1994) claimants who are not considered ILO unemployed either because they combine benefit with more than one hour of work (332,000) or are considered 'inactive' because they are either not interested in working, not engaged in job search or not available for work. The unemployment durations of these claimant non-ILO unemployed is unknown.
57. The claimant unemployed duration series, unlike the overall claimant count, is not revised periodically so as to produce a series consistent with the current coverage of the benefit regime.
58. Albeit not sustained because of inter-regional imbalances, mounting inflationary pressures and balance-of-payments disequilibria — hence, not repeatable.
59. This is confirmed by duration estimates by sex from claimant statistics — when uncompleted spells are included — though not when completed spells alone are

considered; see *Employment Gazette*, prior to October 1988. The *Employment Gazette* has now ceased publication of regular series on: duration by age, sex and region and estimates of the likelihood of becoming unemployed and ceasing to be unemployed by age, sex and region.

60. Claimant unemployment, not seasonally-adjusted.
61. These external or 'structural' factors are necessary even if not sufficient conditions for criminality — which also requires subjective elements ('inner' factors such as the breakdown of moral constraints). See Box (1987), Chapter 2.
62. Best measured from the *Labour Force Survey* since the claimant count excludes most unemployed 16 & 17 year-olds who, assumed to be in either work, full-time education or training, are no longer eligible for Income Support.
63. This section draws heavily upon the research of my colleague, David Dickinson (1994).
64. Created using a score based on seven variables, of which three were measures of bad behaviour and the others were: social handicap (including low income, poor housing, and large family size), poor parental child-rearing behaviour, low non-verbal intelligence and convicted parents. See Farrington *et al* (1986), p.348.
65. A recent report from the independent Policy Studies Institute (Kempson *et al* (1994)) includes resorting to petty crime as one (albeit the last) in a hierarchy of actions constituting a survival strategy for low-income households.
66. See Box (1988), Chapter 2.

References

Anderson, S. and Leitch, S. (1994), 'The Scottish Crime Survey 1993: First Results', *Crime and Criminal Justice Research Findings No.1*, April.

Barclay, G.C. (1990), 'The peak age of known offending by males', *Home Office Research Bulletin #28*.

Bonger, W. (1916), *Criminality and Economic Conditions* (Chicago, Little and Brown).

Box, Steven (1987), *Recession, Crime and Punishment* (Basingstoke, Macmillan).

Carr-Hill, Roy and Stern, Nicholas (1979), *Crime, the Police and Criminal Statistics* (London, Academic Press).

Dickinson, David (1994), *Crime and Unemployment* (mimeo, Cambridge Department of Applied Economics).

Farrington, David, P., Gallagher, Bernard, Morley, Lynda, St Ledger, Raymond, J and West, Donald, J. (1986), 'Unemployment, School Leaving and Crime', *British Journal of Criminology*, vol.26, no.4, pps.335-356.

Farrington, D.A. *et.al.* (1988), *Cambridge Study in Delinquent Development: Long-term Follow-up*: Final Report to the Home Office (mimeo, Cambridge Institute of Criminology).

Field, Simon (1990a), 'Trends in Crime and their interpretation: a study of recorded crime in post-war England and Wales', *Home Office Research Study 119* (London, HMSO).

Field, Simon (1990b), 'Crime and Consumption', *Home Office Research Bulletin No.29* pps.5-9.

Freeman, R.B. (1983), 'Crime and Unemployment' in J.Q. Wilson (ed.), *Crime and Public Policy* (California, ICS).

Garman, A., Redmond, G. and Lonsdale, S. (1991), 'Incomes in and out of work: a cohort study of newly-unemployed men and women', *Department of Social Security Research Report # 7*.

Gormally, Brian, Lyner, Olwen, Mulligan, Gerard and Warden, Michael (1991), *Unemployment and Young Offenders in Northern Ireland* (NIACRO).

Kempson, E., Bryson, A. and Rowlingson, K. (1994), *Hard Times? How poor families make ends meet* (London, Policy Studies Institute).

Mannheim, H. (1965), *Comparative Criminology* Vol.2 (London, Routledge).

Mayhew, Pat, Aye Maung, Natalie and Mirrlees-Black, Catriona (1993), *The 1992 British Crime Survey* (London, HMSO).

Northumbria Police (1977), (1978), (1980), *Chief Constable's Report*.

Phillips, M. (1994), 'Power to the people in the war on crime', *The Observer*, 24 April.

Pyle, D.J. and Deadman, D.F. (1994), 'Crime and the business cycle in post-war Britain', *British Journal of Criminology*, Vol.34, No.3, Summer.

Radzinowicz, L. (1971), 'Economic Pressures' in Radzinowicz, L. and Wolgang, M. (eds.), *Crime and Justice* Vol.1 (London, Basic Books).

Reilly, Barry and Witt, Robert (1992), 'Crime and Unemployment in Scotland: an Econometric analysis using regional data', *Scottish Journal of Political Economy*, Vol.39, No.2, May.

Shaw, K. and Lobo, D. (1989), 'Criminal careers of those born in 1953, 1958 and 1963', *Home Office Research Bulletin #27*.

Stevens, Philip and Willis, Carole F., 'Race, Crime and Arrests', *Home Office Research Study* No.58 (London, HMSO).

Tarling, Roger (1982), 'Unemployment and Crime', *Home Office Research Bulletin #14*, pps.28-33.

Timbrell, Martin (1988), 'Does unemployment lead to crime?', *Brookfield Papers #3* (Department of Economics, University of Exeter).

Thomas, D.A. (1925), *Social Aspects of the Business Cycle* (London, Routledge).

Wells, J.R. (1994), 'The Missing Million', *European Labour Forum*, Summer 1994, pps.10-18.

Statistical Sources

Criminal Statistics England & Wales (various)
Employment Gazette
Labour Force Survey
Regional Trends
Scottish Office Statistical Bulletin Criminal Justice Series

APPENDIX
Econometric results

(t-ratios in parentheses)   ** = significantly different from 0 at 1% level   * = significant at 2.5% level

equation #	time period	dependent variable	explanatory variable	constant term	R^2†
1 first difference of logs	1970-92 England & Wales time series	property crime	per cap consumption -2.0** (-6.23)	constant .095** (8.27)	.65
2 first differences of logs	1970-92 England & Wales time series	property crime	per cap GDP -1.97** (-4.40)	constant .082** (6.25)	.48
3 first differences of logs	1970-92 England & Wales time series	property crime	claimant unemployment .14* (2.11)	constant 0.04** (2.58)	.18
4 first differences of logs	1971-92 England & Wales time series	property crime	employment -2.06** (-3.11)	constant .05** (3.97)	.34
5 logs	1992 England & Wales cross-section police force areas	residential burglary	claimant unemployment 1.14** (4.02)	constant 4.52** (7.26)	.29
6 logs	1992 England & Wales cross-section police force areas	theft of a motor vehicle	claimant unemployment 1.30** (4.15)	constant 4.02** (5.85)	.31
7 logs	1992 England & Wales cross-section police force areas	other theft/ unauthorised taking	claimant unemployment 0.55* (2.87)	constant 5.76** (13.69)	.17
8 logs	1992 England & Wales cross-section police force areas	robbery	claimant unemployment 1.77** (3.41)	constant -0.08 (-0.07)	.23
9 logs	1992 England & Wales cross-section police force areas	all burglary plus all theft	claimant unemployment 0.62** (3.45)	constant 7.55** (19.23)	.23
10 absolute change in the variables	1975-92 England & Wales cross-section police force areas	household burglary (per 100,000 population)	unemployment (%) 111.9** (3.55)	constant 377.8** (2.82)	.24
11 absolute change in the variables	1975-92 England & Wales cross-section police force areas	theft of motor vehicle (per 100,000 population)	unemployment (%) 89.6** (2.38)	constant 177.2 (.84)	.13

†R^2 is the measure of the extent to which variation of the left-hand variable, i.e. crime, is explained by the variables on the right-hand side of the equation (unemployment, etc.). R^2 varies between zero and one.

CHAPTER SIX

Employment in Europe

The Annual Survey by the European Commission,
Directorate-General for Employment, Industrial
Relations and Social Affairs

Ken Coates MEP *and Michael Barratt Brown*

The report on Employment in Europe for 1994 continues the detailed annual studies of the employment situation in Europe, which are based on the comprehensive data produced by each member government under the Community Labour Force Survey, directed by Eurostat. Comparisons are then made with similar information from the USA, EFTA and Japan.

In the 1994 report, in addition to the review of trends and prospects of employment, economic growth and labour force participation, more than half of the content is devoted to issues arising from the White Paper on *Growth, Competitiveness, Employment,* published in December 1993. Thus, there are chapters on mobility, labour turnover and labour market flexibility, on changes in working time, on labour costs, social contributions and taxes, on unemployment and labour market policy and on where has job growth and decline occurred?

The report establishes at the outset the situation facing the European Community:

'After three years of recession, little net job creation, and rising unemployment . . . output is recovering and the increase in unemployment seems to have come to an end . . . however . . . the failure of the Community to generate enough jobs to employ all those who wish to work — whether recorded as unemployed or not — is (not) a thing of the past.

'Unemployment remains the major economic problem facing the Community — both now and for the rest of the decade.

'Whether economic growth can be sustained, and whether this can be translated into jobs, depends in part on whether growth of the global economy continues and spreads . . . (in part) on how far the long-standing structural problems identified and analysed in the Commission White Paper on *Growth, Competitiveness, Employment* at the end of 1993 can be overcome.'

These problems were said to be: lack of sufficient co-ordination of economic policy in member states, failure to achieve a sufficiently employment-intensive pattern of growth, insufficient flexibility of labour markets, and inadequate investment in education and training.

They were accompanied by *increasing divergencies in incomes and job opportunities between those in strong positions in the labour market and those in weak positions,* and by limited progress in convergence of living standards and job opportunities between people living in different regions of the Union.

The White Paper's proposed strategy to tackle these problems had two basic elements: better coordination of national economic policies and more employment-intensive patterns of production. The strategy was endorsed at the European Council meetings in Brussels in December 1993 and confirmed in Corfu in June 1994, when the Council identified seven key areas for particular attention:

● improving flexibility within enterprises and in the labour market;
● reorganisation of work at the enterprise level;
● targeted reductions in the indirect costs of labour especially statutory contributions and especially of unskilled labour;
● better use of public funds set aside for combating unemployment;
● developing employment in new areas of activity;
● specific measures aimed at young people without adequate training;
● improving education and training systems.

The Employment Report for 1994 addresses the first five of these 'key areas'; but it begins with a review of the scale of the employment challenge in the Community and the relationship between output growth and employment growth over the long term in the Community and elsewhere, and gives particular attention to examining why employment in the Community is much lower relative to working-age population than elsewhere — *a 58% participation rate compared with 70% in the USA and Japan, 68% in EFTA.*

I
Employment developments

The following are the chief findings about employment trends:

1. Over the past 30 years the labour force in the Community grew by 30 million (25 million women: 5 million men); half was matched by an increase in employment half by a rise in unemployment.

2. In 1994 there were some 18 million unemployed in the Community (including 1 million in the new Laender in Germany) according to the Community Labour Force Survey (LFS), but 4 million of these were not registered as such by the respective national employment offices. At an unemployment rate of 11%, this is higher than EFTA (8%), USA (7%) and Japan (3%).

3. Economic growth of 1½% in 1994 and 2½% in 1995 could not prevent employment from falling in 1994 or achieve more than a very modest increase in 1995. Unemployment was higher in 1994 (May) than in 1990 in all twelve countries, especially for women (in the UK alone, the rate for men was higher than the rate for women).

4. *There is considerable hidden unemployment not only among women, but also among older people persuaded to retire early.* Women's participation rates have increased especially among the 25 to 49 age group, but men's rates have declined even among that prime age group and especially among those under 25 and over 55. This is not only because of extended years of education at the bottom end, but because people effectively disappeared from the labour force during the recession. Only 6% of men aged 65 and over were still economically active in the Community in 1992 compared with 15% of this age group in the USA and 40% in Japan.

5. *The growth in the participation of women has been the main reason for labour force growth everywhere in the Western world. Women's participation rate in the Community rose from 34% in 1960 to 67% in 1992, but this is still below the 75% rate in EFTA and the USA.* The growth has been particularly marked in those countries of the Community — Spain, Ireland, Germany and the Netherlands — where participation of women was initially comparatively low.

6. Economic growth in the developed countries resulting from increases in productivity has slowed down markedly since the mid-1970s, especially from reduced productivity growth in the non-manufacturing sector. The Community's experience has been similar to that in the USA, EFTA and Japan, but, while productivity growth in manufacturing in the Community has been maintained, this has been at a lower level of productivity than in other developed regions, which implies less competitiveness; and in recent years productivity growth in manufacturing in the USA has been rising again.

7. Low or nil productivity growth in the non-manufacturing sector has meant that this sector could absorb the loss of jobs in manufacturing; and even a reduced rate of output growth could still lead to some increase in employment. *Employment in services in the Community has risen from 43% in 1965 to 64% in 1993, 55%*

for men, 78% for women. The services share is highest of all the twelve countries in the UK, especially for men.

8. Growth of employment throughout the developed countries has risen very much in line with growth in GDP over the past 30 years, with ups and downs of growth according to the trade cycle, but with generally lesser amplitudes in employment. These ups and downs have, however, been very much greater in the UK, where alone of all the 12, and of the countries in EFTA, the US and Japan, up until 1991-2 there were actual declines in GDP. These occurred in the UK in 1975, 1979-81, 1989-92, and in manufacturing value added they resulted in falls of the order of 4% to 8% in 1980 and 1991, with cuts in employment of 8% to 10%. *These sharp checks to growth were the main cause of the UK's slower rate of growth over the period and higher average rate of unemployment.*

9. Real wages in manufacturing industry in the Community have risen in line with the growth of labour productivity, but because of the relatively lower rates of productivity growth in the Community, unit labour costs have risen at twice the rate of those in the US and Japan over the years 1970 to 1991. *This implies a steady deterioration in cost competitiveness, which has had to be compensated for by exchange rate depreciation.*

10. There have also been major variations in unit labour costs and inflation between member states of the Community as well as between the Community and other developed countries. The rise in the UK and in Italy of unit labour costs at about 10% a year over the period 1971-1991, compared with only 4% a year for Germany, had to be compensated for by exchange rate adjustments. Such adjustments are not costless, since they raise import prices for the country devaluing its currency, and this must itself fuel inflation.

II
Follow-up to the White Paper on Growth, Competitiveness, Employment

The following are the main findings:

1. *Changes in employment* conceal much larger movements of people into and out of work and between jobs, which all contribute to the flexibility necessary to meet changing demand. Years of low net job creation tend to be associated more with a high rate of job loss than a low rate of new recruitment. *Flexibility does not appear to be associated with more rapid economic growth.* Countries with higher rates of unemployment have higher rates of labour turnover.

2. *Labour turnover* is made up of movements between sectors, movements within sectors and movements from unemployment or inactivity into employment, the last making up about 60% of the total. The highest rates of turnover are found among women and in the services sector, most particularly in banking and finance. Chances of movement decline with age. In the years between 1984 and 1992 about one in nine of those in employment had taken on a new job in the preceding year, but in 1992 the LFS showed that one in six had not been in the same job a year earlier. The figure for labour turnover over the whole period was highest in the UK, where growth was the weakest, and lowest in Germany where growth was strongest.

3. There is some evidence that *investment in training tends to be discouraged if labour turnover is high* since firms financing the training are less sure of recouping the benefits. Germany and Belgium with low sectoral mobility have a developed labour market structure with investment in training a key element.

4. The main change in *working time* over the period, 1983-1992, was a reduction in full-time working hours for both men and women employees of between one and two hours a week. In 1983 51% of men worked 40 hours a week and 16% 37-39 hours; by 1992 the figures were respectively 29% and 36%. *However, the proportion of men working over 40 hours remained at 23% and over 48 hours rose from 10% to 12%.* While in most countries of the Community the normal working week is between 38 and 40 hours, in the UK 55% of the men worked more than 40 hours a week in 1992, 28% over 48 hours. Most *women* in the Community work less than 40 hours and, while 10% worked more, in a few countries, including the UK, about that proportion worked under 10 hours. In the Community as a whole, 31% of women regarded themselves as part-time workers.

5. A considerable proportion of men and some women were found in 1992 to be working *unsocial hours.* Five million men (7%) and 2 million women (3%) normally worked nights while a further 11% of men and 5% of women sometimes did so. The proportions occasionally working at night and sometimes working on a Saturday were much higher in the UK than in other Member States (over 40% for men and women), suggesting more flexible working time arrangements.

6. *Social contributions* paid by *employers* — both statutory and voluntary — do not seem to be much different in the Community and in the USA, respectively 22% and 21% of total labour costs, but both are above the Japanese figure of 15%. Wage levels appear to take account of employers' social contributions, so that the Paper

concludes 'that reducing their contribution to the cost of social protection in Europe would not necessarily benefit European producers as much as it might seem . . .'

7. Differences between the Community and the USA and Japan seem to be greater in respect of *employees' contributions and taxes on wages.* These averaged out in the Community to a figure of some 20% of labour costs, compared with 10%-15% in the USA and Japan. Thus in the Community in 1991 employers' and employees' tax, etc., payments for a male worker in manufacturing amounted to 45% of labour costs.

8. Social contributions and taxes vary greatly between countries in the Community, higher employers' contributions often being balanced by lower employees' payments and vice versa. The Netherlands, Denmark, Belgium and Germany are found at the top end, Portugal, Spain and the UK at the bottom end. *The 'League Table' for social contributions is thus found to be almost the exact reverse of that to be found in respect of growth in GDP and employment.*

9. *Tax rates* in the Community are progressive, the rate rising as incomes rise, and in the UK contributions are also progressive. Thus the higher the pay, the more goes to the state; and, since women's pay is lower than men's — on average 28% less than men's for manual workers in manufacturing in 1991 — the social costs of employing women are less. Indeed, in the UK social contributions are not required for women working less than 15 hours a week. For full time workers, the flat rate of social contributions in all countries except the UK means that non-wage labour costs imposed by government bear proportionately more on workers at the lower end of the scale.

10. The *marginal tax rate* is an important consideration for workers considering entry to employment. A progressive tax system can mean that taxes and employee's contributions take as much as 50% of extra earnings in moving up from 80% to average earnings levels. 50% is the Community average. In the USA the take is 40% and in Japan 30%. Compared with these figures, the UK has the lowest marginal tax rate of all Community countries — at just over 40%. *Very low social contributions and taxes at lower earnings levels in the USA mean that employers there can employ workers at little more than take home pay.* This applies also to part-time women workers in the UK.

11. Low wages implies *poverty.* If poverty is defined for a household as one receiving less than 50% of the average for all households, then towards the end of the 1980s, 10% of all Community households where there was at least one member at

work — 7½ million in all comprising some 19 million people — were in poverty. *Taken together with the pensioners, this is one third of the households in poverty.* The major cause of poverty was old age in all countries except the UK and Ireland, where it was unemployment. This was just true also in Belgium and Netherlands, where less than 7% were in poverty compared with 17% in the UK and Ireland. Over the Community as a whole, moreover, the chances of a household falling below the poverty line were 4 times greater on average, if the head of the household was unemployed.

12. *Unemployment* has been a central problem for all states in the Community (except for Luxemburg), but the nature of the problem has been changing. *Young people* under 25 accounted for 34% of the unemployed in 1985 but for only 32% in 1994. This is partly the result of demographic changes (falling birth rates), partly because young people stay on longer in education, but chiefly because unemployment of young women only rose very slightly in the recession of the 1990s. The rate for young men rose sharply — by over 5% of the labour force. *Unemployment among the under 25s remains at around 20% for both men and women*, compared with 11% and 8% respectively for women and men over 25. Youth unemployment rates are particularly high in the southern states — Greece, Italy and Spain — and in Ireland, where the proportion of young people in the population remains high.

13. *Long term unemployment* was the second major characteristic of the unemployment of the early 1980s, but seemed to be less serious as overall unemployment rose in the early 1980s, those who had been out of work for more than a year falling from 52% of the total in 1985 to 43% in 1992. *The proportion can be expected to have risen since 1992.* The problem of the long term unemployed is particularly serious in the South and in Ireland where it is combined with long term unemployment among the youth. In the North the problem of long term unemployment mainly affects the old, but the UK also has a combination of long term unemployment among the youth.

14. *Methods of seeking work* vary greatly between different countries in the Community. 80-90% in France, Germany and Spain use the public employment offices and almost as many in the Netherlands. Less than 15% do in Ireland and Greece, and the next fewest are in Portugal and the UK where only just over 30% use such public offices. Most in these countries rely on the press, together with the grapevine of friends and relatives. This is particularly the case with women. There is evidence of significant decline in the use of public employment offices, associated with the

decline in the proportion of the unemployed registering at these offices, as the rules for registration have been tightened.

15. Public *labour market expenditure* in the Community on passively supporting those who cannot find work or more pro-actively increasing their employability amounted in 1992 to about 3% of Community GDP for the member states taken together. Over half of this sum went on paying income support and another 10% on funding early retirement schemes. *That left 40% — no more than 1% of Community GDP — for active measures of training, job subsidies and employment services.* Denmark spent the most (over 6%) as a proportion of GDP on active as well as passive policies, followed by Germany and Ireland. Spain and the UK spent about 3%, mostly on passive policies. Luxemburg, Greece, Spain and the UK spent least on active policies, under half of one per cent.

16. Expenditure on *labour market policies per unemployed person* varies even more widely in the Community — between 30-40,000 ecus in 1992 in Luxemburg, the Netherlands and Denmark, most of it on active measures, and under 5,000 ecus in Spain, Portugal, Greece, Italy and the UK, most of it on passive support. Expenditure per unemployed person on active measures actually declined in the early 1990s, except in Germany, the Netherlands and Portugal. The UK real spending on training per person unemployed was halved in 1991-3.

17. In a careful statement on 'employment systems in member states' the report outlines the many reasons — historical and cultural background, economic levels of development and social circumstances — for the wide diversity in member states' employment systems. It emphasises the need to assess efficiency, learn from others' experiences, open up the European labour market, encourage women's participation, and avoid conflicts of standards and especially any temptation to engage in a competitive lowering of standards.

18. A final section examines the *structure of employment* across the Community and the areas of job growth as they have been revealed since 1985 and as they may be anticipated in the future. The decline of agriculture and the rise of the service industries are well known and widely experienced throughout the Community. Only in Greece, Portugal and Ireland does agriculture account for more than 10% of the working population. Services account for around two thirds of all employment. Distribution, hotels and catering provide 20% of the jobs in all countries, finance and business services another 10%, public administration about 7%, transport and communications about 5%, and 'other services' varying proportions depending on the share of education and

health, ranging in all from 30% (Denmark) to 15% (Greece). The UK has a particular high proportion of jobs in retailing, largely because of the large number of part-time women working average hours 10% lower than elsewhere in the Community.

19. One outstanding difference in the mix of employments throughout the Community is to be found in the high share of employment in engineering and metal manufacture in Germany, at 15% over twice the average for the Community as a whole. This is exceptional even in relation to the US, Japan and EFTA. *Almost 40% of all workers in these metal working industries in the Community work in Germany.* By contrast the share of services in German employment is relatively low, but has been increasing faster than elsewhere since the mid-1980s.

20. In most countries of the Community between 1985 and 1990 the service industries, particularly the business services accounted for nearly the whole of the total growth of employment. This growth in service employment was maintained during the next three years at a lower rate, while the industries which had shown some growth previously — office machinery, mechanical engineering, rubber, plastics and construction and to a lesser extent motor vehicles, paper and printing, timber and wood — were all hit by the recession. It seems that in the last two years cuts have reached the service sector, particularly in business services and transport.

21. Experience in the USA, Japan and EFTA has been similar to that in the Community. Growth in employment in the 1970s and 1980s was nearly all in services. Employment in agriculture in the USA was stationary, while there was some slight growth in industry. In Japan the decline in agriculture was rapid and growth in industry slight. In Europe, while services grew, both industries and agriculture declined. This failure of industry bodes ill for the future, as the recession ends. *The report argues that, while industry cannot be regarded as a major direct source of employment growth in future years, employment losses in industry would have a multiplier effect on service employment.*

22. *Changes in occupations and skills* have been concentrated mainly in the continuing increase in employment for professional and technical workers. Whereas these only comprised 15% of all jobs in 1983, they provided 40% of the increase in jobs over the next eight years, thereby rising to 25% of all jobs. This growth continued into the 1990s when by contrast the earlier growth in clerical and related jobs ceased. Production and related jobs having increased in the mid 1980s were also sharply cut back during the recession. Jobs in agriculture continued to decline throughout the 1980s. *It appears that in the periods of low employment and output*

*growth, the shift in jobs towards professional and technical workers
was much more pronounced than in the high growth years.* In these
low growth periods it is the lower grade jobs which tend to be cut
back and consequently the less skilled workers who suffer most job
loss. What is said here about more and less skilled jobs applies
equally to men and women, although men have suffered more from
cuts in production and related jobs and women in clerical jobs
during the periods of recession.

23. *Small and medium sized firms have been responsible for
much of the growth in employment in the Community in the past.*
This is for the very good reason that in the private sector, most
people work in small firms — 55% in firms with under 100
employees, 30% in those with under 10. This is not only true in
services, where 60% work in firms with under 100 employees and
36% with under 10. The comparative figures in manufacturing are
40% and 12%. Contrary to the general view, figures for small firms
in manufacturing industry in Japan are even larger than they are in
the Community — 56% in firms in Japanese manufacturing with
under 100 employees. Small firms are especially important in
manufacturing in southern Europe, not so much because of
sub-contracting as in Japan but because of the less developed nature
of manufacturing in those countries and the relative weight in them
of industries such as clothing and footwear. In services small firms
predominate everywhere in Europe, except for the UK and Belgium
where *the small shop is being rapidly ousted by the wide spread of
the multiple stores.*

CHAPTER SEVEN

Opening the Drawer Marked 'Forget'

Ken Coates MEP

At the beginning of this little book we argued that it is impossible that mass unemployment can cohabit with social justice. The only justice which is admitted in this cruel universe is very primitive: raw, red in tooth and claw.

Unfortunately, it seems that modern fashions in social theory seek to obtain a form of justice which is blind to the miseries of the poor, and deaf to the appeals of those who lack work.

While the unemployment statistics ran away into their second and third millions under the Thatcher administration, the Labour Party in Britain was historically associated with the crusade for full employment. John Prescott captured this commitment in his manifesto for the Labour Party's leadership election in May 1994. He deliberately sought to reassert the firm engagements made by the late John Smith, who had embraced full employment as his own prime goal, when he sought the leadership in 1992.

For the first twenty-five post-war years, Prescott insisted in his appeal for Labour votes, 'unemployment never rose above two per cent'. However, in the 1970s it doubled, and under the rule of Mrs Thatcher, it trebled. 'Over the past fifteen years claimant unemployment has averaged 2.4 million . . . and in both recessions it has topped three million. This cannot go on.'

John Prescott was right about this, and he was right to say that 'unemployment is a moral outrage that should not be tolerated'. Prescott had previously had the occasion to explore possible remedies at the level of the British economy, and we shall look at these in a moment. It is enough to say, here, that he encountered some obstacles in his pursuit of appropriate forms of action. Perhaps that is why, in 1994, he made the firm promise:

'If I am elected as Leader of the Labour Party, I will immediately establish a Commission for Full Employment to report to the 1995 Labour Party Conference, alongside the Commission on Social Justice, established by John Smith.

The Commission for Full Employment could look at the changes that are necessary to develop a job creation programme if full employment is made the key economic priority it deserves. Its remit would be to:
● define full employment and achievable employment targets in a modern economy
● establish a proper basis for measuring levels of employment and unemployment
● conduct a wide-ranging review of the medium-term and long-term social and economic policies needed to achieve full employment.
● establish a proper basis for a social productivity analysis of local employment
● assess how European resources can best be used to complement and assist local, regional and national jobs programmes
● establish the criteria for a jobs audit
● establish a national skills audit.'

There is much to be said for such a Commission, although it would be more likely to succeed if it were established at the European level, and enabled to work across a whole area of the European Community. In any case, there is obviously some resistance to this agenda in the Labour Party itself. This perception is reinforced by Mr Prescott's own experience, as a Shadow Employment Minister in the time of Neil Kinnock.

On the 6th February 1987, *The Guardian* reported John Prescott as

'urging Labour to create 1.5 million new jobs in the first two years of a new administration, using local authorities as the main generator of employment. The sort of jobs envisaged include street cleaners, bus drivers, health care workers, loft insulation teams and local enterprise initiatives. In political terms a policy which tells local authorities to increase their spending is not an obvious election winner. However, this is only part of a much wider industrial strategy to be debated by Labour.'

The original goal of creating one million jobs had not been a foolish or empty target. It had enlarged itself, because of the continuing erosion of existing jobs. Mr Prescott acknowledged this problem, giving it as his own belief 'that it may be necessary to create 1.5 million new jobs in order to take one million people off the unemployment register.'

This was reported in *The Guardian* of the 13th February 1987, with a bold promise.

'"These jobs will be spelled out, in the most detailed exercise of this kind ever carried out by an opposition party," he said. Mr Prescott has already prepared a pamphlet, *Real Needs — Local Jobs*, which urges the shadow cabinet to give local authorities substantial powers to create jobs as part of the Labour commitment. It also envisages a substantial upheaval in relations

between Whitehall departments and between central and local government.
A behind-the-scenes argument took place during its production, with
Mr Prescott having to make revisions.'

On the 15th February 1987, *The Times* reported:

'Labour's performance last week illustrated its leadership malaise. On
Sunday, John Prescott, Labour's employment spokesman, floundered
on ITV's *Weekend World* on the crucial question of how Labour intends
to fulfil its pledge to get a million people off the unemployment register.
On Wedneday, *The Times* reported that Kinnock had made Bryan Gould,
his campaign co-ordinator, overall boss of Labour's jobs package. On
Thursday, Prescott was forced to admit to jeering Tory MPs that Gould
was indeed in charge of the cash bags for jobs.

The secret shuffle had been decided in January, but . . . had leaked.
Prescott's one success last week was to insist against the whip's advice
that Labour MPs be put on a three-line whip for Thursday's debate on
employment and training. The result was that 160 Labour MPs were
kept at Westminster to witness his discomfiture. But not Neil Kinnock.
He was a notable and unexplained absentee, as were Roy Hattersley,
Denis Healey and John Cunningham.'

The very week before, Mr Nigel Lawson had proposed to
introduce tax cuts, which were estimated to involve £3 billion. The
Labour Party argued that £3 billion pushed into the economy
through such cuts, releasing private expenditure, would create only
40,000 jobs, whereas targeted public expenditure could create
300,000 jobs.

The targeting of such public expenditure was envisaged as falling
mainly within the Local Government sector.

Of course, just as John Prescott lost his responsibility for
unemployment, Labour lost the 1987 General Election. Its recovery
did not begin in earnest until the election of John Smith, who was
seen as a man of integrity, but who was also determined to deal
with mass unemployment.

Neither in 1987 nor in 1992 was the Labour Party willing to centre
its campaign on precise proposals to end unemployment. John
Prescott's brief period of responsibility marked the high point in the
efforts of the Labour front bench to grapple with Britain's most acute
social crisis: and in retrospect the decision to replace him can be
seen to have been a tragic one.

It is very interesting that in 1995, the General Municipal and
Boilermakers' Union found that its search for a credible full
employment strategy led straight towards Regional Government.
In accents very reminiscent of John Prescott's earlier, doomed,
initiative, the Union insists that 'the prime purpose of Regional
Government should be economic regeneration'. Different regions

Table 1
GMB: distribution by region of jobs to be created

Region	Production jobs	Public service jobs	Production service jobs
South East	28,000	30,000	55,000
East Anglia	6,600	5,600	980
London	20,000	37,000	76,960
South West	14,760	15,400	26,500
West Midlands	26,800	17,400	28,500
East Midlands	18,300	12,270	19,440
Yorks and Humberside	22,000	18,100	28,730
North West	26,000	23,070	38,000
Northern	16,000	14,300	19,000
Wales	10,800	10,600	14,000
Scotland	19,000	20,500	29,100
Total	208,260	204,240	336,210

experience different problems, and 'require different strategies'. This marks out a strong case for devolution, since regeneration decisions are most likely to optimise the allocation of resources, 'combining targeting and economies of scale'.

In a fascinating exercise, the Union assumes a target 'to eliminate unemployment within the country'. They further assume that the new jobs created would follow the distribution of existing jobs, between production, public and private services. And they estimate, for the sake of argument, that a third of the jobs to be created overall will depend upon Regional Government initiatives. This gives them a breakdown which is described in Table 1.

All this will serve to focus minds. If the Labour Party, or any other Party in Britain were determined to defeat unemployment, it would be necessary to mobilise now, in order to ensure that all the relevant resources could be tapped in time to install new policies with a change of Government. Prescott's earlier political intuition was right: the policy on this vital matter can be encouraged and fostered by the centre, but will depend on willing collaborators at every different level of administration. Unfortunately, this insight was not understood, or not accepted, as continuing policy by the Kinnock team.

The truth is that the Labour Party enjoyed but one brief interval of commitment to full employment, after the 1992 General Election, when John Smith took over the leadership. He came out to Strasbourg on the campaign trail, and talked to a group of Labour MEPs who had been agitating for a European Recovery Programme, to prioritise action against unemployment. He told us that he wholeheartedly approved of these objectives. We believed him, and came to see Smith as a refreshing change, since he was capable of remaining loyal to the same commitments from one year to the next.

In 1993, he reiterated this commitment, and told the Trade Union Congress in Brighton that he supported both full employment and a national minimum wage.

Jon Sopel, the biographer of Tony Blair, tells us that this remarkably effective speech did not please everybody. 'To the modernisers', he says, 'it smelt like a sell out'. 'Blair', he claims 'was furious. The speech seemed to him a hostage to fortune that would saddle Labour with policies it could never realistically sell to the electorate . . . Kinnock was aghast, too.'

For the unemployed, the death of John Smith was an overpowering blow. This was the context in which John Prescott campaigned for the Labour leadership, and made the commitment to a Commission for Full Employment, which is described above. Jon Sopel tells us that the prospects for such a Commission are no better than were Prescott's earlier prospects in the time of Mr Kinnock. He reports that Prescott 'was determined that Labour should go into (the) Election with a . . . promise to slice the jobless totals. This is something Labour refused to do in either the 1987 or 1992 General Election, and it is something that is likely to have a veil drawn over it, or be put in some far away pending tray, marked "forget".'

In other words, the question to be resolved in the British political space is not how to restore full employment, but whether to make the effort. It is, alas, perfectly thinkable that we could have a new Labour Government which accorded full employment no priority whatever, and sought, instead, to juggle the existing figures, within tighter or narrower margins, greater or lesser ameliorative measures. Such an option would ensure that the excluded society not only continued, but continued in deterioration.

The commitment to full employment clearly requires a co-ordinated action, from the level of the European Union down to the regional and local levels which were involved in Mr Prescott's initiative. Such co-ordination would make powerful demands on national governments, who would need to act resolutely to remove the obstacles to joint and combined action in the European Union, whilst at the same time fostering the creative energy and resoures of local and community action.

We shall treat on some of these eminently practical questions in a companion volume to this little book, *Putting Europe Back to Work.*

European Recovery Programme Essential for Full Employment

A full-blooded European Recovery Programme of joint action by all the states of the European Community is essential to restoring full employment in Europe. It needs to be urged forward by their common institutions, and to emphasize reductions in working time.

In the circumstances of the 1990s, such joint action for economic recovery should naturally be led by the European Commission, and co-ordinated with member governments.

a
EUROPEAN
RECOVERY PROGRAMME
Edited by
KEN COATES MEP &
MICHAEL BARRATT BROWN
Contributors include
Francis Cripps ● Jacques Delors ● Wynne Godley ● Stuart Holland ● John Hughes ● Allan Larsson ● Sir Donald MacDougall ● Andrew Marvell ● Regan Scott ● Peter Townsend ● Terry Ward

This book proposes a detailed framework for a recovery programme and seeks to prove that mass unemployment is not at all inevitable and can be overcome. It will be of interest to trade unionists and all those concerned with the crisis in employment and social provision.

A European Recovery Programme: Restoring Full Employment, edited by Ken Coates MEP and Michael Barratt Brown.
□ **ALLAN LARSSON MP** Can Europe Afford To Work? □ **KEN COATES** MEP The Dimensions of Recovery □ **MICHAEL BARRATT BROWN** Money, Debt & Slump □ **JACQUES DELORS** The Scope and Limits of Community Action □ **SIR DONALD MACDOUGALL** Economic and Monetary Union and the Community Budget □ **ANDREW MARVELL** Funding the Recovery Programme □ **STUART HOLLAND** Planning the Recovery Programme □ **PROF. WYNNE GODLEY** A Federal Government? □ **PROF. PETER TOWNSEND** What Hopes for European Social Policy? □ **FRANCIS CRIPPS & TERRY WARD** Employment Creation □ **MICHAEL BARRATT BROWN** Regional Recovery □ **REGAN SCOTT** Reforming Working Lifetimes □ **JOHN HUGHES** Linking Working Time with Recovery □ **KEN COATES** MEP Afterword: An Assize on Unemployment and Poverty? □

"It is vital that the debate about these and other ideas in the battle for jobs is taken out now to the people and our regional and local communities".
Ken Coates